beans

beans

*Seventy-nine
Recipes for
Beans,
Lentils,
Peas,
Peanuts,
and Other
Legumes*

Bonnie Tandy Leblang
and Joanne Lamb Hayes

Harmony Books/New York

Published by Harmony Books, a division of Crown Publishers, Inc., 201 East 50th Street, New York, New York 10022. Member of the Crown Publishing Group.

Random House, Inc. New York, Toronto, London, Sydney, Auckland

HARMONY and colophon are trademarks of Crown Publishers, Inc.

Manufactured in the U.S.A.

Designed by Linda Kocur

Illustrated by Jennifer Harper

Library of Congress Cataloging-in-Publication Data

Leblang, Bonnie Tandy.
Beans : seventy-nine recipes for beans, lentils, peas, peanuts, and other legumes / Bonnie Tandy Leblang and Joanne Lamb Hayes. — 1st ed.
p.   cm.
Includes index.
1. Cookery (Beans)   2. Cookery (Legumes)   I. Hayes, Joanne Lamb. II. Title.
TX803.B4L43   1994
641.6′565—dc20   93-4433
CIP

ISBN 0-517-59203-7

10   9   8   7   6   5   4   3   2   1

First Edition

contents

acknowledgments

Thanks—

to Kathy Belden, who was instrumental in the conception of this book and without whose vision it would not be;

to Jerry Munson and Jim Melban from the California Dry Bean Advisory Board and Sue Hays from the American Dry Bean Board for technical assistance;

and as always, thanks to Eric, Bryan, Claire, and Heather for their loving support.

introduction

Beans are a fun food. When you mention beans to most people, a smile comes to their face. Whether brought by the remembrance of Grandma's molassesy home-baked beans basking in the oven awaiting a New England Saturday night supper, a tin plateful of barbecued beans hot and tomato-steamy from a campfire Dutch oven, a novice meal cooked over a hot plate in your first studio apartment, or just one of the world's many bean jokes, beans make people happy.

They are always reliable, friendly, down-to-earth, good people-food, and now we are finding out that they are good for us as well.

While most people love beans, until recently they have been associated with lean times. Despite the fact that this high-energy carbohydrate fueled the founding of America, provided the energy with which the West was won, and nourished our nation through depressions and wars, beans have been typecast as the staple diet of the poor. But not anymore. High in soluble fiber, available in dozens of colorful varieties, and appearing on menus in all the best places, beans are writing a new chapter in their millennia of history. The nineties is the decade of the bean.

Our biggest problem in writing this book was deciding which of the thousands of wonderful bean dishes to include. We have enjoyed reproducing family favorites as well as discovering new tastes. Bean versatility excites the imagination, and we could have gone on forever. We hope your family and friends will enjoy our choices as much as ours have.

bean biography

Long before adventurers in sailing ships tied the continents together with trading routes and scrambled the world's food supply, each third of the globe was cultivating, perfecting, and enjoying its own special bean. In Asia, the soybean became an important staple protein in the diet, appearing as cooked beans, sprouts, oil, salted and fermented beans, and pressed curds (tofu). The garbanzo and the broad (fava or feve) bean, cultivated in Europe and North Africa since antiquity, are the beans mentioned in the Bible and in the works of Roman writers. In all parts of the Western Hemisphere, haricot (from the Aztec *ayacotl*) beans were cultivated in a wide range of varieties, each suited to the particular climate in which it was raised. The late fifteenth and early sixteenth centuries saw a rapid exchange of people, products, and ideas between these three different bean-growing areas. The result—bean culture was changed forever.

Early colonists to North America found the indigenous

population living on a combination of beans, maize (corn), and squash with only the occasional addition of fish or game. Archaeological evidence from several Mexican sites shows that this "three sisters" diet (maize, beans, and squash) sustained a large population by 2000 B.C. Native Americans taught the colonists how to cultivate the three crops together. Years of experience had taught them to fertilize the neat rows of corn by planting fish with the seeds. Bean seeds were planted between the corn seeds so that the bean plants could be trained to climb the cornstalks for support. Broad-leaved squashes were planted between the rows of corn. They shaded the earth, keeping the moisture in and preventing weeds from getting the light they needed to grow. From the beginning, beans were an important factor in the survival of European communities in the New World.

Everywhere that beans traveled, they became a part of the traditional foodways of the area. Not just an occasional item on the menu, they staked out a position of importance in the hearts of the people. In combination with the local foods of an area, beans formed the basis of many of the national dishes of Europe, Africa, and Asia. It is no surprise that when people from these areas moved to America, their bean dishes accompanied them. Today, Americans enjoy legumes in a rainbow of colorful, flavorful, and comforting combinations. This book reflects both the international character of the bean dishes we have discovered around us and the personal bean memories of our childhood.

bean nutrition

Beans are a nutritional powerhouse, chock-full of not only

protein, complex carbohydrates, and fiber, but also many vitamins and minerals. Compared to other high-protein foods, beans are low in calories—on average a cup of beans provides about 225 calories. Beans have no cholesterol and minimal fat. (Soybeans are the one exception, with 43 percent of their calories from fat.)

Although beans are an excellent and inexpensive source of protein, the protein is incomplete. Like other plant sources of food, they are missing or low in an amino acid, an essential part of proteins that the body cannot make. Specifically, beans are low in methionine. The key to getting the *most* from beans or other plant foods is to combine them to make a complete protein. By serving beans with grains (cereal, rice, corn, or pasta), seeds, nuts, or a small amount of an animal food source (meat, fish, poultry, eggs, cheese, milk)

the available protein is complete or balanced. Some examples include Red Beans and Rice, Hummus, and Pasta e Fagioli (see pages 103, 44, and 32).

Beans are one of the best sources of dietary fiber, providing up to 14 grams per cup of cooked beans. Beans are rich with vitamins and minerals. They're an abundant source of B vitamins, including niacin, thiamin, riboflavin, B_6, and folacin. In general they're also a good source of calcium, iron, zinc, potassium, and other trace minerals. The kinds and amounts of minerals and vitamins vary with the type of bean. That's a good enough reason, as any, to keep on hand and use a variety of beans.

Beans are a good nondairy calcium source for those unable to drink or allergic to milk. Iron from vegetable sources, like beans, is not as easily absorbed as that from animal sources. To help the body absorb the plant iron more effectively, eat beans along with vitamin C–rich foods (tomatoes, green pepper, broccoli, or citrus juices, such as lemon, lime, orange, or grapefruit).

The U.S. Department of Health and Human Services, the National Cancer Institute, the American Heart Association, the Surgeon General, and other health organizations all agree we should eat less fat, more complex carbohydrates, more fiber, and fewer calories. Beans fit that bill without breaking the bank.

bean glossary

Adzuki: A small (¼-inch) oval, russet-colored dry bean with a white line along its ridge. This bush bean has a nutty sweet flavor and soft texture. It's eaten fresh, dried, sprouted, and ground into flour. Associated with Oriental foods. *Also known as:* aduki, azuki.

Anasazi: A bean said to have been grown by the Anasazi Indians for at least one thousand years, now beginning to appear on the market.

Antique Beans: Ancient varieties of beans that are being returned to small commercial production by boutique growers.

Appaloosa: A dappled red-and-white bean resembling the markings of an Appaloosa pony. Interchangeable with pink, pinto, or small red bean. Available dried.

Bean: Generic name for legumes used in this book. See *Legumes* for botanically correct definition.

Bean Flakes: Partially cooked, rolled, and dried beans made into flakes in order to cook faster.

Bean Flour: Pulverized or ground beans. Garbanzo and soy flours are the most common.

Bean Pasta: Usually made from mung beans.

Bean Sprouts: The offshoot of beans, usually adzuki, mung, or soy, forced to germinate by storage in a warm, moist place.

Black Bean: A medium (⅝-inch) kidney-shaped black-colored dry bean with a white keel and an earthy-mushroomy flavor. Available canned, dried, and rehydrated. Associated with South American, Caribbean, and Mexican foods. *Also known as:* turtle beans.

Black-eyed Pea: A medium (½-inch) kidney-shaped off-white dry pea with a purplish-black color on its keel. It has a sweet pealike, earthy flavor and a buttery smooth texture. Available canned, dried, frozen, and rehydrated. *Also known as:* brown-eye peas, blackeye beans, blackeyes, cowpeas, and purple-eyes.

Broad Bean: See Fava.

Butter Bean: See Lima Bean.

Cannellini Bean: A medium (½-inch) oval white-colored dry bean with a slightly nutty flavor and smooth texture. Available canned and dried. *Also known as:* haricot blanc, white kidney bean.

Chick-Pea: See Garbanzo.

Christmas Bean: A large, flat, red and white mottled bean. One of the most popular of the "antique" beans returning to production, it closely resembles large lima beans in flavor and texture.

Cranberry Bean: A medium (½-inch) oval, plump, tannish-pink dry bean with wine-colored mottling, which turns pink on cooking. Its mild, sweet nutlike

beans and health

Current research suggests that eating beans is beneficial in terms of cardiovascular health and cancer prevention. Researchers have linked bean's soluble fiber to a reduction of the "bad" cholesterol—the low-density lipoproteins or LDL cholesterol, while the American Cancer Society now suggests eating beans, as well as other high-fiber foods, to help reduce the risk of cancer.

Beans, which are rich in both fiber and complex carbohydrates, are digested more slowly than other high-fiber foods. This slow digestion is advantageous to both insulin-dependent diabetics and to those trying to lose weight. For diabetics, less insulin is needed to control blood sugar levels after a meal of beans than after one of other carbohydrate foods. For the overweight, this slow digestion translates into a much longer feeling of fullness than when other foods are eaten, often resulting in weight loss.

flavor is similar to that of the pinto bean. Available dried and fresh in season. *Also known as:* borlotti, Roman, Rosecoco, shelly bean.

Dal: A generic name used for legumes in India.

Decorticated: The term to indicate that the husk or outer shell is removed from the bean.

Fava: A large (¾- to 1¼-inch) oval, tan-colored dry bean. The fresh bean is pale green in color. Assertive, almost bitter earthy flavor and granular texture. A tough-skinned bean, it is often served as puree. Available fresh in spring, dried, and canned.

The fresh kernels should be peeled before cooking. *Also known as:* broad bean, faba, feve, horse bean.

Flageolet: A medium (½-inch) kidney-shaped, pastel green–colored dry bean. A delicacy because the immature kidney bean is removed from the pod when young and tender. Fresh tasting. The most expensive of all beans. Available dried, fresh, and canned.

Garbanzo: A small (⅜-inch) knobby, round-shaped, buff-colored dry pea. It has a nutty, somewhat chestnutty, taste and a firm texture. Available canned, dried, and rehydrated. *Also known as:* ceci, chick-pea.

Great Northern Bean: See White Beans.

Haricot: Phaseolus vulgaris, the bean indigenous to the Western Hemisphere. The name derives from the Aztec name, *ayacotl.* French term used for bean.

Favism is an inherited allergylike reaction to the eating of undercooked fava beans and in some cases to the plant's pollen. People of Mediterranean background (the ancestral homeland of fava beans) are most susceptible.

Kidney Bean: A medium (½-inch) kidney-shaped dry bean in two colors, liver red or light red. A robust flavor and creamy texture. The mature seed of a variety of green beans that when picked immature produces the delicate flageolets. Interchangeable with red beans in recipes. Available dried and canned. *Also known as:* chili bean, habichuela, haricot rouge, Mexican bean.

Legumes: Dry beans, peas, and lentils that belong to the *Leguminosae* family. Legumes are the edible mature seeds inside pods.

8

Lentil: A very small (¼-inch) flattened disk or lens-shaped dried seed of a small shrub. Can be many colors including brown, green, or red. Lentils have a light fresh flavor and firm texture. No need to soak lentils; they are quick cooking. But watch closely near the end of cooking since they soften easily and tend to disintegrate. Available dried.

Lima Bean: A (½- to 1¼-inch) light green bean, creamy white with a pastel green tint when dry. Has a buttery flavor and a creamy texture. Available canned, dried, fresh, and frozen. Should always be cooked before eating. *Also known as:* butter, Madagascar, sieva beans.

Methionine: The essential amino acid missing in beans, making the protein incomplete. Combine beans with other protein foods containing methionine, such as cheese, meat, seeds, nuts, rice, or

bean digestion

There's no getting around it, beans have the reputation of being "the musical fruit." Because they contain oligosaccharides, complex sugars not digested by the body, they provide for the gas-producing bacteria in the lower intestine. Some people are more affected than others. Many find that continued consumption of beans allows the body to adjust to oligosaccharides in the diet. Proper soaking and cooking reduces the problem considerably. Although our mothers taught us to use the soaking and cooking liquid from beans so as not to lose the vitamins it contains, we prefer to waste the vitamins along with the oligosaccharides that have come out into the cooking liquid, and enjoy more digestible beans.

other grains, to complement the bean's protein value.

Mung: A small (¼-inch) green, brown, or black roundish dry bean, with a somewhat sweet flavor and soft texture. These beans are sprouted to produce bean sprouts, which even contain vitamin C, not found in the dry bean. Available dried, ground into flour, or canned or as fresh bean sprouts. *Also known as:* black gram, green gram, golden gram, *moong dal,* split golden gram.

Navy Bean: A small (¼-inch) oval white dry bean with a mild flavor and mealy texture. Interchangeable with other white beans such as Great Northern. *Also known as:* haricot bean, pea bean.

Oligosaccharide: An indigestible complex carbohydrate (polysaccharide) present in beans, which often causes flatulence.

---

help for gas problems?

A bean book wouldn't be complete without a mention of the food enzyme (alpha-galactosidase) sold in supermarkets and pharmacies under the name Beano. The food enzyme breaks down oligosaccharides, the indigestible sugars in beans that cause bloating and/or flatulence. To use, just add a few drops of the liquid enzyme to your first bite of beans.

We've found that Beano works for some, not for all. What does work is eating beans more frequently. The more beans you eat, the less gas you have.

Pea: A small (¼- to ⅜-inch) round gray-green dry bean with an earthy sweet flavor and soft texture. Another variety is available fresh, canned, frozen, or dried. *Also known as:* mar-rowfat, field pea. See also Split Peas.

Pea Bean: See Navy Bean.

Peanut: A tan pod containing two tan oval seeds covered with a papery mahogany-colored skin. Not a bean at all, but a legume. Available in the shell or shelled, roasted or unroasted, salted or unsalted, and ground into pea-nut butter. *Also known as:* earth nut, groundnut, monkey nut, goober.

Pigeon Pea: A small (¼-inch) tan-colored round dry bean with a pungent flavor and mealy tex-ture. Available both dried and canned. *Also known as:* Congo Pea.

Pink Bean: A pale pinkish-brown bean similar to the small red kidney bean with a meaty flavor and mealy texture. Inter-changeable with red bean, small kidney bean, or pinto bean.

Pinto Bean: A small (⅜-inch) oval beige and pinkish-brown mottled dry bean with an earthy flavor and mealy texture. Avail-able dried and canned.

Pulses: A generic name for le-gumes: beans, lentils, and peas. The seeds of leguminous plants.

Quick Soak: A method used to rehydrate beans quickly, when you forgot to let them soak over-night (see page 20). We recom-mend the salt soak (see page 19).

Red Bean: A small (⅜-inch) bean, somewhat oval shaped, with the same liver red color of the dark kidney bean. It has a robust flavor and creamy tex-ture. Interchangeable with kid-ney beans in recipes. Available dried or canned. *Also known as:* small red bean.

Rehydrated Beans: Dry beans soaked in a salt solution until the beans absorb much of the moisture. Currently only a few varieties are sold in plastic bags in the produce department.

Salt Soak: A method for rehydrating beans in salted water, using about 1 to 2 teaspoons salt to 1 pound beans (see page 19).

Soluble Fiber: The indigestible part of plant foods, such as beans, lentils, and peas, which easily dissolves in water.

Soybean: A small (⅜-inch) round bean with a crisp, mild nutlike flavor and firm texture. Usually pale ivory or yellow in color, but also can be black, brown, or green. *Also known as:* soya beans, soy peas.

Split Peas: Peas that are husked and split in half. Can be green or yellow and have a more earthy flavor than the unsplit peas. Available dried.

Tempeh: Fermented soy product, rich in protein.

Tepary Bean: A bean of Mexican origin, similar to the haricot bean, just beginning to be available. Use in place of white beans.

Tofu: A firm or soft custardlike product, made by grinding cooked soybeans with liquid, then curdling and pressing as is done with cheese.

White Beans: The mature seeds of varieties of green beans. This includes Great Northern, marrow fat, navy, pea, and small white beans.

Winged Beans: Long green or reddish beans with four winglike ridges along the sides. Sometimes called the bean of the future because all parts of the plant can be used for food.

bean timing

There's no exact science to cooking beans since they are a product of nature—as well as of handling. The longer beans are stored, the more moisture they are likely to lose. Warm storage temperatures will also reduce their moisture, while high-humidity storage will actually increase it. So, beans that have been stored for an extended period of time in a warm, dry climate will take longer to cook than fresh dry beans or those stored in humid climates.

How can you tell how fresh the beans are? You can't be sure. You can purchase beans from a store with a high turnover of products—but other than that, you should test the beans for doneness and not be surprised if they are not cooked in the suggested amount of time. The beans you cook this week might take up to one hour more to soften than the ones you prepared last week. First test a bean for doneness by squeezing a bean between your fingers—if it yields to pressure easily, then taste it to see if it's done.

Most of the recipes in *Beans* call for already cooked beans because of their unpredictable cooking time.

bean equivalents

1 pound dry beans = about 2 cups dry beans = about 6 cups cooked

½ pound dry beans = about 1 cup dry beans = about 3 cups cooked

One 20-ounce can cooked beans = about 2 cups, drained

1 cup cooked beans = about 1 cup mashed beans

2 to 3 tablespoons dry beans = 1½ to 2 cups sprouts

troubleshooting

If your beans are too firm:

● *the beans had been stored too long—cook them longer than usual.*

● *the beans had been stored in a hot, dry place—cook them longer than usual.*

● *you didn't soak or cook them long enough.*

● *the concentration of salt in your cooking liquid was too high—add salt late in cooking period or count on longer cooking.*

● *you added acid (like tomatoes, lemon juice, or wine) too early in the cooking period—wait to add high-acid ingredients until beans are almost tender.*

● *your water is too hard (high in minerals)—try using distilled water.*

If your beans are too mushy:

● *you cooked them too long—because cooking time varies, be sure to check beans frequently for tenderness.*

● *you soaked them longer than usual and didn't reduce cooking time to compensate.*

● *you added baking soda—adding baking soda to soaking or cooking water causes beans to soften faster, but we don't recommend it because it is very difficult to control.*

If your beans lose their skins during cooking:

● *you used the quick soak method or cooked them without soaking—longer soaking allows the whole bean to expand at the same rate and reduces splitting and skin loss.*

● *you boiled them too rapidly—a gently simmer reduces splitting and skin loss.*

● *you cooled them after draining—beans resist cracking better if cooled in water.*

If your beans are flavorless:

● *you did not add enough salt—salt is essential for bean flavor. You can use less total salt if they are salt soaked.*

If your pot of beans tends to foam and boil over:

● *your pot is too small—leave at least 2 inches headroom above water level.*

● *your heat is too high—cook beans over low heat.*

● *add a teaspoon or two of oil to the pot to reduce foaming.*

basic
bean
recipes

I will arise and go

now, and go to

Innisfree,

And a small cabin

build there, of clay

and wattles made:

Nine bean-rows will I

have there, a hive for

the honey bee. . . .

—W. B. YEATS,

The Lake Isle of

Innisfree, 1899

Legumes are very versatile vegetables. They may be eaten when immature, mature, or dry. In each of these stages, they are traditionally used in different dishes and are handled differently. Frequently, different varieties are planted for each of three stages of use.

When immature, beans are cooked in their pods for a short period of time and served as a side dish or as a part of a main dish. Snow peas and sugar snap peas are used in the same way.

In mature beans and peas, the pod has dried out and the kernels are enlarged and fleshy. To prepare, the pods are removed and discarded and the kernels are cooked for an intermediate period of time, depending upon the variety and maturity of the bean or pea. They are usually served in the same ways as immature beans.

Dry beans or peas have been allowed to stay on the plant un-

Our favorite dry bean strategy is to salt soak the beans overnight, cook them completely, drain them well, and freeze them in 1- or 2-cup packages. If you have a selection of cooked beans in the freezer, a quick dinner is only minutes away. The frozen beans can be thawed in the microwave or stirred, still frozen, into a simmering soup, sauce, or stew.

til both the pod and the kernel have become very dry. They are removed from the shell and often stored for a period of time before use. Depending upon the variety and the amount of time they have been stored, they must be soaked before cooking and need a long cooking period to become tender. Dry beans, lentils, or peas often provide both the protein and carbohydrate in a meal and appear as a part of the main dish. Because dry beans are more complicated to cook than the rest, and because the majority of the recipes in this book include dry beans, we will explore their preparation first.

dry beans

One pound makes about 6 cups cooked

soaking

All dry beans need to be soaked to rehydrate them before cooking—dry lentils and peas do not. We tested all the methods of soaking that we knew and found that we preferred a slow salt soak. The beans rehydrated more evenly, needed less salt in final preparation, and had better skin retention when cooked. The only consideration with this method is that it takes time—preferably 6 to 8 hours or overnight. We recommend refrigerating beans for both of the slow methods because they begin to ferment if held in a warm place for a long time.

First, pick through beans and discard any discolored or shriveled beans and foreign matter. Rinse the beans well and place them in a 5-quart bowl or saucepan. Then select one of these soaking methods:

slow salt soak: Add 10 cups water and 2 teaspoons salt to 1 pound of beans. Set aside to cool to room temperature. Cover tightly and refrigerate 6 to 8 hours or overnight.

traditional slow soak: Add 10 cups water to 1 pound of beans. Set aside to cool to room temperature. Cover tightly and refrigerate 6 to 8 hours or overnight.

hot soak: In a 5-quart saucepan, heat 10 cups water to boiling. Add 1 pound of beans. Bring to a boil over high heat; remove from heat; cover tightly and set aside at room temperature 2 to 3 hours.

quick soak: In a 5-quart saucepan, heat 10 cups water to boiling. Add 1 pound of beans. Bring to a boil over high heat; let boil 2 to 3 minutes. Cover tightly and set aside at room temperature 1 hour.

cooking

■ 1. Discard soaking water and rinse beans well in a colander. Place beans in a 5-quart saucepan or Dutch oven. If using dry lentils or peas, pick through and rinse before placing them in the saucepan. Add 8 cups water, 1 tablespoon olive or other vegetable oil, and 1 teaspoon salt (see note).

■ 2. Bring the bean mixture to a boil over high heat; reduce heat, cover partially with a tilted lid, and cook until desired tenderness. The cooking time will vary with the variety of bean, length of time beans have been stored, temperature of storage area, and the soaking method you have selected.

■ 3. When beans, lentils, or peas are done, drain and use in the recipes that follow or immerse completely in cold water until cool; drain well and freeze in 1- to 2-cup packages for later use.

note: *Beans will cook faster if salt is not added, but will need addition of more salt in the final recipe. For more savory beans, you can add 1 small onion, quartered, 2 garlic cloves, ¼ teaspoon ground black pepper, and ½ to 1 teaspoon of herbs such as thyme, basil, oregano, or dill at this point.*

oven method: Heat oven to 350° F. Follow directions above, combine beans, hot water, oil, and salt in a 5-quart, ovenproof casserole with lid, or Dutch oven. Bring to a boil, place on a

20

rimmed baking sheet, and bake until desired tenderness.

pressure cooker method: Using one of the above methods, soak ½ pound beans, or sort and rinse ½ pound peas or lentils. In a 4-quart pressure cooker, combine the prepared beans, peas, or lentils, 4 cups water, 1 teaspoon oil, and salt to taste, if desired. Cook at 15 pounds pressure following manufacturer's directions for the type of legume you are cooking. Cooking times will vary from 3 to 4 minutes for lentils and peas to 10 to 12 minutes for soybeans. Always reduce the pressure rapidly under cool running water when cooking beans, peas, and lentils to prevent overcooking.

Quick-cooking beans will take 10 to 12 minutes, medium cooking beans will take 15 to 18 minutes, and long cooking beans, about 25 minutes.

note: *Because dry beans need long, slow cooking to rehydrate, microwaving is not a practical and time-saving method for cooking them. It can be done, but unless there is a reason why it is necessary to cook them in the microwave, other methods are just as fast and energy efficient.*

note: *You can substitute canned beans for cooked beans in our recipes. Just rinse and drain before using. Be sure to reduce the amount of salt you use when substituting canned beans.*

note: *Rehydrated beans are now available in the produce section of your supermarket. They have been salt soaked and are ready to be cooked. Be sure to follow package directions for cooking time.*

fresh green, yellow (wax), italian, french, long, and winged beans

Makes about 4 servings

1 pound fresh green,
  yellow (wax), Italian,
  French, long, or winged
  beans

1. Bring 3 cups of water to boiling in a 3-quart saucepan or large skillet over high heat.
2. Rinse beans well. Snip off stem ends and if dried or if you prefer, pointed tip. Trim off both ends of winged beans.
3. Cut French or long beans into 4-inch pieces; cut Italian and winged beans into 2-inch pieces. If green and yellow beans are mature, they should be cut diagonally crosswise into 2- to 3-inch pieces or Frenched (split lengthwise).
4. Add beans to boiling water; return to boiling. Cover, reduce heat, and cook 5 to 7 minutes for tender young green or yellow beans, French beans, Frenched beans, and long beans; 8 to 10 minutes for mature beans and Italian beans; and 15 minutes for winged beans, or to desired tenderness (see note).

note: *Desired tenderness varies greatly across the country. Although very few people use the old-fashioned, boil-them-an-hour method, our cooking times may be a bit too crisp- tender for some people.*

microwave method: *Prepare beans according to steps 2 and 3 of recipe above. Place in 1½-quart casserole with ½ cup water and salt to taste. Cover tightly and microwave on full power (100 percent) for times as listed in step 4 above. Stir once, halfway through cooking time. Remove from heat and let stand, covered, 5 minutes.*

fresh kernel beans, lima beans, and peas

Makes about 4 servings

3 pounds fresh kernel
  beans, lima beans, or
  peas
3 cups water
Salt and freshly ground
  black pepper to taste
Butter (optional)

1. Shell beans or peas. Bring water to a boil in a 2-quart saucepan over high heat.
2. Add beans or peas to boiling water; return to boiling. Cover, reduce heat, and cook 25 to 35 minutes for kernel beans, 20 to 30 minutes for limas, or 8 to 10 minutes for peas.
3. Drain well; add salt and pepper. Toss with butter, if desired, and turn into serving dish.

leftover bean bonus

Whenever you cook up a batch of beans, prepare at least twice as much as you need. Pack the cooked beans in 1- to 2-cup portions in freezer bags or containers. Be sure to label the bag with the type of bean, the date, and the amount in the bag. When you're ready to cook, add the frozen beans as is to stews or soups, but defrost them first for salads. To defrost quickly, add water to cover to the container and microwave on full-power (100 percent) for 1 to 2 minutes, let stand 1 minute, then drain.

bonus number 2— a thickener

Use mashed beans as a thickener. When you have leftover beans, mash or puree, then freeze in ice cube trays. Once frozen, pop from the trays and store in a freezer container or bag. No need to defrost—just add directly to your soup, stew, or sauce.

guide for substituting

With few exceptions, practically any bean can be used for any cooking purpose. But to get similar results, use a suggestion from this substitution guide. Otherwise, just have fun experimenting.

when a recipe calls for: **substitute:**

cranberry beans	*pinto beans*
kidney beans	*red beans*
pinto beans	*cranberry, small kidney, pink or red beans*
red beans	*kidney beans*
white beans	*cannellini, Great Northern, pea, or navy beans*

soups

If pale beans

bubble for you

in an earthenware

pot, you can

oft decline the

dinners of

sumptuous hosts.

—Martial, *Epigrams,*

A.D. 86–102

black bean soup

Using fully cooked ham and pre-cooked or canned beans, you can prepare this hearty soup in under a half hour.

6 servings

1. Cut ham steak into ½-inch pieces; reserve bone. Heat the oil over medium heat in a heavy, 4-quart saucepan. Add the ham pieces and the bone, onion, and garlic and sauté, stirring constantly, until the onion is golden, about 5 minutes.
2. Add the water, carrots, beans, salt, and pepper. Bring to a boil, reduce heat to low, and cook 15 to 20 minutes or until the carrots are just tender.
3. Add the spinach. Return to boiling over high heat; cook 3 to 5 minutes or until spinach has wilted. Remove ham bone before serving.

vegetarian variation: *Omit the ham steak.*

1 pound fully cooked bone-in ham steak

1 tablespoon olive oil

1 medium onion, chopped (about 1 cup)

2 garlic cloves, minced

8 cups water

2 medium carrots, sliced (about ½ cup)

3 cups cooked black beans (pages 19–21), drained

Salt and freshly ground black pepper to taste

½ pound spinach, rinsed very well and torn into bite-size pieces

effie's fassoulada

This version of the traditional Greek soup was inspired by the one Effie Tandy often makes.

8 servings

1. Heat the oil in a heavy, 6-quart saucepan or Dutch oven. Add the onions and garlic and sauté until golden, stirring constantly, about 5 minutes.
2. Stir in the water, tomatoes, beans, and pepper. Bring to a boil over high heat; reduce heat to low, cover, and simmer 1½ hours. Add the mint and salt; simmer 15 minutes longer or until beans are tender.

⅓ cup olive oil

2 large onions, chopped (about 3 cups)

2 garlic cloves, minced

2½ quarts water

1 16-ounce can crushed tomatoes

2 cups Great Northern beans, picked over and soaked (pages 19–20)

Freshly ground black pepper to taste

1 sprig fresh mint or ½ teaspoon dried

Salt to taste

---

cracked pepper

For a more intense pepper flavor, we often use cracked pepper instead of finely ground. You can purchase cracked pepper in a jar from the supermarket spice section or crack your own by setting your pepper mill on coarse grind.

---

escarole and fagioli soup

Soup needn't take hours to prepare. Here's an example of one that can be on the table in less than 15 minutes.

4 servings

1. Heat the oil in a 2-quart saucepan. Add the salt pork and sauté until it releases its fat and begins to brown. Stir in the escarole, cover, and let cook 3 to 5 minutes, until the leaves wilt.
2. Season with hot pepper flakes. Add the beans, water, salt, and pepper. Bring to a boil, lower the heat, and simmer 5 minutes. Taste and adjust seasoning.
3. Serve with lots of pepper and Parmesan.

variation: *Substitute 1 pound fresh spinach for the escarole. Or use a 10-ounce package frozen spinach and add along with the beans.*

vegetarian variation: *Omit the salt pork and add 1 teaspoon Tabasco or other hot pepper sauce.*

1 tablespoon olive oil

¼ cup diced salt pork or bacon

1 head escarole, rinsed well and torn into bite-sized pieces

Pinch hot pepper flakes

½ cup cooked white beans (pages 19–21), drained

2 cups water

Salt and freshly ground black pepper to taste

Freshly grated Parmesan cheese

grandma little's buttersoup

When Ellen Schoen Brockman was a child, her Grandma Little made this hearty soup for her. Ellen, a friend of Bonnie's, loved buttersoup better than candy, cake, or cookies. We love it too. Our adapted version, like most soups, is even better the second day!

4 to 6 servings

1. In a 4-quart saucepan over medium-high heat, combine lima beans, carrots, celery, tomatoes, and water. Bring to a boil, reduce heat, and simmer, partially covered, until beans are tender, about 1 hour.

2. In a small skillet over very low heat, melt all but 1 teaspoon butter. Add onion and parsley and cook until onion is soft, about 5 minutes. Stir in flour until smooth. Add to simmering soup, stirring constantly, until blended. In same skillet over high heat, melt the remaining butter and cook the pasta until golden, about 3 minutes. Add to the soup, season with salt and pepper, and simmer until the pasta is cooked through, about 5 minutes.

1 cup dry lima beans, picked over and soaked (pages 19–20)

2 small carrots, finely chopped (about ¾ cup)

2 large celery ribs, finely chopped (about 1⅓ cups)

1 cup chopped, drained tomatoes

6 cups water

3 tablespoons butter

1 small onion, finely chopped (about ½ cup)

2 tablespoons chopped fresh parsley

2 tablespoons all-purpose flour

2 tablespoons pastina or other tiny pasta

Salt and freshly ground black pepper to taste

golden portuguese bean soup

Shelly Johnson, Bonnie's sister, provided the inspiration for this hot, spicy, and satisfying soup that's rich in beta carotene.

6 to 8 servings

1. Pierce the sausages with a fork. Poach in boiling water for 5 minutes. Drain and slice into ¼-inch rounds. **2.** Cook the sausages in a 4-quart saucepan over medium-high heat until lightly browned, about 5 minutes. Add the onion and cook until golden, about 5 minutes. Add the water, squash, sweet potatoes, carrots, cracked pepper, salt, and pepper flakes. Bring to a boil, reduce heat, cover, and simmer for 20 minutes.

The recipe can be made ahead up to this point. Refrigerate until ready to continue.

3. Add the beans and cabbage. Simmer, covered, an additional 10 minutes. Taste and adjust seasoning.

1 pound Portuguese or other garlic sausage, such as linguiça

1 large onion, minced (about 1½ cups)

6 cups water

1 butternut squash, peeled, seeded, and diced (about 3 cups)

2 medium sweet potatoes, peeled and diced (about 3 cups)

4 carrots, diced (about 2 cups)

½ teaspoon cracked black pepper

¼ to ½ teaspoon salt, to taste

¼ to ½ teaspoon hot pepper flakes, to taste

2 cups cooked kidney beans (pages 19–21), drained

1 small head green cabbage, cored and chopped (about ½ to ¾ pound)

vegetarian variation: *Omit sausage. Cook the onion and 2 cloves minced garlic in 1 tablespoon oil until the onion is golden, about 5 minutes. Continue with recipe.*

Senate bean soup, a ham bone–flavored, senate stand-by potato-thickened navy bean soup, has been served in the U.S. Senate dining room since early in this century. When once it disappeared from the menu, a bill was introduced on the floor of the Senate mandating that the soup be included on the menu every day that the dining room is open.

pasta e fagioli

Here's a simplified version of an old hearty Italian favorite. Instead of cooking each component separately, they're all prepared in one pot, leaving you with less cleanup!

6 servings

1. Heat the oil in a heavy-bottomed 2-quart saucepan over medium heat. Add the onions and cook, stirring occasionally, until softened, about 5 minutes. Add the garlic, celery, squash, and carrots and cook, stirring frequently, for 3 minutes.

2. Add the beans, water, and oregano. Bring to a boil over high heat, reduce heat to low, cover, and simmer for 1 hour, or until beans are tender. Add the tomatoes and salt. Cook, covered, 10 minutes.

The recipe can be made ahead until this point. Refrigerate until ready to continue.

3. Bring to a boil, stir in macaroni, reduce heat, and simmer, covered, for 5 minutes. Remove from heat, add 1 cup Parmesan cheese, and let stand 5 minutes before serving. Taste and adjust seasoning. Serve with additional parsley, if desired, and cheese.

1 teaspoon olive oil

2 medium onions, sliced (about 2 cups)

2 garlic cloves, minced

2 celery ribs, chopped (about 1⅓ cups)

1 medium zucchini or yellow squash, chunked (about 1 cup)

3 carrots, sliced (about 1½ cups)

1 cup dry white beans, picked over and soaked (pages 19–20)

4 cups water

1 tablespoon dried oregano

3 medium tomatoes, peeled, seeded, and chopped (about 2 cups) *or* 2 cups drained canned chopped tomatoes

1 teaspoon salt or to taste

1 cup dried macaroni

1 cup freshly grated Parmesan cheese, plus additional for the table

Chopped fresh parsley (optional)

quick minestrone soup

With a quick glance, this may seem to have a long list of ingredients. But basically, it's just some beans and pasta, with lots of vegetables and seasonings, cooked in a broth.

8 appetizer servings; 4 entree servings

1. Heat the oil in a 4-quart saucepan over medium-high heat. Add the onion and sauté until softened, about 5 minutes. Stir in carrots, celery, garlic, basil, and oregano. Then add the broth, bring to a boil, reduce heat, and simmer 5 minutes.
2. Add the sherry, zucchini, tomatoes, green beans, kidney beans, and fusilli. Simmer an additional 10 to 15 minutes or until pasta is cooked. Season with salt and pepper. Taste and adjust seasoning. Stir in Parmesan just before serving.
3. Serve with additional Parmesan cheese at the table, if desired.

2 tablespoons olive oil

1 medium onion, sliced (about 1 cup)

2 carrots, sliced (about 1 cup)

2 celery ribs, coarsely chopped (about 1⅓ cups)

2 garlic cloves, minced

2 teaspoons dried basil

1 teaspoon dried oregano

6 cups vegetable or chicken broth

⅓ cup dry sherry

1 medium zucchini, chunked (about 1 cup)

2 medium tomatoes, peeled, seeded, and diced *or* 1½ cups canned crushed tomatoes

¼ pound fresh green beans, cut into 2-inch pieces

2 cups cooked kidney beans (pages 19–21), drained

¾ cup fusilli (spiral) pasta

Salt and freshly ground black pepper to taste

½ cup freshly grated Parmesan cheese, plus additional for the table

mulligatawny soup

6 to 8 servings

1. Heat the butter in a 4-quart sauce-pan over low heat. Add the onion, garlic, curry, salt, hot pepper flakes, and black pepper and sauté until the onion is softened, stirring constantly, about 5 minutes.

2. Add the broth, lentils, and coconut. Bring to a boil, reduce heat, and simmer about 40 minutes, stirring occasionally. Allow soup to cool slightly.

3. Add lime juice. Process in a blender or food processor by pulsing a few times to puree, but not until smooth.

The recipe can be made ahead until this point. Refrigerate until ready to continue.

2 tablespoons butter

1 large onion, chopped (about 1½ cups)

2 garlic cloves, minced

3 to 4 teaspoons hot curry powder, to taste, *or* 1 teaspoon each ground coriander and turmeric, ½ teaspoon each ground ginger, dry mustard, and freshly ground black pepper

1 teaspoon salt

¼ teaspoon hot pepper flakes

Freshly ground black pepper to taste

2 quarts chicken or vegetable broth

1 cup lentils, picked over and rinsed

¼ cup grated coconut

¼ cup freshly squeezed lime juice

Low-fat yogurt

Grated lime zest

4. Reheat before serving. Taste and adjust seasoning. Garnish with a dollop of plain low-fat yogurt sprinkled with lime zest.

variation: *For a quicker and chunkier version, do not process the soup in the blender or food processor.*

pesto vegetable soup

Although you may not think of soup in the summer, this one's delightful as light fare on a cool summer's eve. It's stocked with lots of fresh vegetables and redolent of fresh basil. Just add a crusty bread to complete the meal.

8 to 10 servings

1. Heat the oil in a 4-quart saucepan over medium-high heat. Add the onion and sauté until golden, stirring constantly, about 5 minutes. Stir in the carrots, zucchini, and yellow squash. Then add the water, beans, tomatoes, parsley, salt, and pepper. Bring to a boil, reduce heat, and simmer for 40 minutes.

The recipe can be made ahead up to this point. Refrigerate until ready to continue.

2. Meanwhile, make the pesto by pureeing the Parmesan, basil, and garlic in a food processor or blender. With the machine running, slowly add the oil until a paste forms.
3. Stir half the pesto into the soup and remove from the heat. Taste and adjust seasoning. Serve immediately, with the additional pesto.

soup

1 teaspoon olive oil

1 medium onion, chopped (about 1 cup)

3 carrots, chopped (about 1½ cups)

1 medium zucchini, chunked (about 1 cup)

1 medium yellow squash, chunked (about 1 cup)

2 quarts water

2 cups cooked white beans (pages 19–21), drained

3 medium tomatoes, peeled, seeded, and chopped (about 2 cups) *or* 2 cups drained canned chopped tomatoes

2 tablespoons chopped fresh parsley

Salt and freshly ground black pepper to taste

pesto

1 cup freshly grated Parmesan cheese

⅓ to ½ cup fresh basil leaves, to taste

3 garlic cloves

¼ cup olive oil

classic pesto

Pesto gets its name from the Italian pestare, *meaning to pound. Long before the arrival of food processors, Italian cooks were pounding together fresh basil, garlic, pignoli, and olive oil to toss with their homemade pasta. Many people feel that the processor-chopped version will never match the flavor of the original.*

To make pesto, for each serving, pound 1 garlic clove and ¼ teaspoon salt in a large mortar with pestle until it makes a paste. Add 1 cup chopped fresh basil, ½ cup chopped fresh parsley, and, if desired, 1 tablespoon pignoli or chopped walnuts. Pound together, gradually adding ¼ cup flavorful olive oil until a smooth sauce forms. Stir in 2 to 4 tablespoons freshly grated Parmesan cheese, if desired but not necessary. To serve, stir in a tablespoonful of pasta cooking water and toss with 8 ounces dried pasta, cooked and drained.

ribollito

Ribollito is Italian for reboiled. In this quick-to-make soup, you add mashed, already cooked beans—hence the name. This addition not only thickens the soup but turns it into an extraordinarily hearty, stick-to-the-ribs soup.

6 servings

1. Heat the oil in a 4-quart saucepan over medium-high heat. Add the onion and sauté until softened, about 5 minutes. Stir in the garlic, parsley, thyme, and rosemary and cook an additional minute. Stir in the celery, carrots, and tomato puree.

2. In a bowl, using a fork or in a food processor, mash 1 cup beans. Add the mashed beans and the water to the saucepan. Bring to a boil, reduce heat, and simmer, covered, 15 minutes.

The recipe can be made ahead until this point. Refrigerate until ready to continue.

3. Add squash and remaining 3 cups beans. Simmer 10 minutes. Remove from heat, season with salt and pepper, stir in Parmesan cheese, and let stand a few minutes before serving. Serve with additional Parmesan cheese at the table, if desired.

2 tablespoons extra-virgin olive oil

1 large onion, chopped (about 1½ cups)

4 garlic cloves, minced

2 tablespoons chopped fresh parsley

1 teaspoon dried thyme

1 teaspoon dried rosemary

2 celery ribs, coarsely chopped (about 1⅓ cups)

2 carrots, coarsely chopped (about 1 cup)

2 cups tomato puree

4 cups cooked white beans (pages 19–21), drained

4 cups water

1 large yellow squash, coarsely chunked (about 2 cups)

Salt and freshly ground black pepper to taste

¾ cup freshly grated Parmesan cheese, plus additional for the table

three pea soup

The addition of fresh peas and pea pods gives a new twist to this split pea soup.

4 servings

1. Heat the oil in a heavy 3-quart saucepan over medium heat. Add the onion and garlic and sauté, stirring constantly, until the onion is golden, about 5 minutes.

2. Add the water and split peas. Bring to a boil, reduce heat to low, and cook 35 to 40 minutes, uncovered, stirring occasionally, until the peas are soft. Measure the mixture and add water, if necessary, to make 4 cups.

3. Beat the half-and-half into the flour with a wire whisk. Beat the mixture into the soup and cook, beating constantly until the soup thickens and the peas break up. Add salt and pepper.

4. Add the fresh green peas; return to a boil over high heat; cook 8 to 10 minutes or until the peas are tender. Stir in the snow peas; if necessary, add water until the soup reaches the desired consistency. Return to a boil; taste and adjust seasoning; serve.

1 tablespoon olive oil

1 medium onion, chopped (about 1 cup)

2 cloves, minced garlic

6 cups water

1½ cups split green or yellow peas, sorted and rinsed

½ cup half-and-half

1 tablespoon all-purpose flour

Salt and freshly ground black pepper to taste

1 cup fresh or frozen green peas

¼ pound snow peas, strings removed and cut crosswise into 1-inch pieces

starters

I never met anybody

so full of beans.

—J. B. PRIESTLEY, *The Old*

Dark House, 1928

adzuki pâté

These tiny red beans of Asian origin are packed with nutrition. Their nutty flavor makes this chunky dip a hit.

4 to 6 servings

1. In a medium bowl, with a potato masher or a fork, mash the beans with the soy sauce, chopped pepper, and ginger, until pureed but not smooth.
2. Spoon into a small serving dish and top with scallion. Serve with sesame crackers.

2 cups cooked adzuki beans (see pages 19–21), drained

1 tablespoon soy sauce

2 tablespoons finely chopped green bell pepper

½ teaspoon ground ginger

1 scallion, finely chopped (about 2 tablespoons)

Sesame crackers

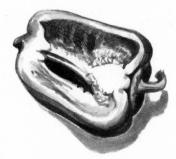

country caviar

Serve these pickled black-eyed peas as an appetizer, a side dish, or a dressing over garden lettuce.

4 servings

1. In a medium bowl, whisk together the vinegar, sugar, salt, black pepper, and cloves.

2. Stir in the black-eyed peas, bell pepper, and scallions. Cover and refrigerate at least 2 hours to marinate before serving. Serve chilled.

¼ cup cider vinegar

1½ tablespoons sugar

Salt and freshly ground black pepper to taste

⅛ teaspoon ground cloves

2 cups cooked black-eyed peas (see pages 19–21), drained

½ medium red bell pepper, cored, seeded, and finely chopped (generous ⅓ cup)

2 scallions, finely chopped (about ¼ cup)

hummus bi tahini

Adjust the consistency of this lem-
mony hummus by adding water or additional lemon juice. Use it thick as a
dip for fresh vegetables or pita, but
thin it with a few tablespoons of liquid for use as a sauce over falafel
(page 94).

4 to 6 servings

2 cups cooked garbanzos
(chick-peas; pages
19–21), drained

3 garlic cloves, minced

¼ cup sesame seed paste
(tahini)

6 tablespoons freshly
squeezed lemon juice

¼ cup freshly minced
parsley

Pinch of salt

1. In a food processor or blender,
combine the garbanzos, garlic, sesame
paste, lemon juice, parsley, and salt.
Process until smooth.
2. Taste and adjust seasoning.

low fat bean dip

Bean dips needn't be laden with fat calories. This one's not.

4 to 6 servings

1. In a small saucepan, mash the beans with the onion, liquid, jalapeño peppers, chili powder, salt, and cumin, then warm over low heat. Place into a ramekin or other bowl. **2.** Serve at room temperature or slightly warmed. If desired, top with cheese and broil for 2 minutes, until the cheese melts, before serving with tortilla chips.

note: *Be sure to wash your hands after handling jalapeño peppers. The pepper's volatile oils could burn your skin or eyes.*

2 cups cooked pinto beans (pages 19–21), drained

½ small onion, finely chopped (about ¼ cup)

2 tablespoons bean cooking liquid or water

1 to 2 jalapeño peppers to taste, seeded and minced (see note)

2 teaspoons chili powder

½ teaspoon salt

½ teaspoon ground cumin

Shredded Monterey Jack regular, light or jalapeño cheese (optional)

Tortilla chips

quick quick
bean dip

What could be quicker than combining cooked beans with your favorite salsa or picante sauce? No need to chop jalapeño peppers to increase the heat—just choose a hot salsa to begin with. This is sure to become a favorite to whip up when unexpected company comes. If you keep already cooked beans frozen in 1- or 2-cup portions as we strongly recommend, you'll always be ready to make this or most other bean recipes.

4 servings

2 cups cooked beans
 (pages 19–21), drained

16-ounce jar mild,
 medium, or hot salsa

Tortilla chips

1. In a small bowl, partially mash the beans, using a fork. Mix in the salsa.
2. Serve with your favorite tortilla chips.

---

salsa

There are almost as many recipes for salsa as there are people who like to eat it!

To make a bowlful, just combine some chopped fresh tomatoes (peeled or unpeeled) with finely chopped onions (or shallots or scallions), minced jalapeño peppers (or mild or hot green chilies), chopped fresh parsley (or cilantro), and freshly squeezed lemon or lime juice. If desired, add some minced garlic, salt, and pepper.

Just vary the quantity and ingredients to suit your taste.

quick
southwestern
bean dip

When you have a bit more time, instead of mashing the beans, just toss them with your favorite salsa, along with some corn, fresh peppers, and cilantro.

8 to 10 servings

1. In a small bowl, combine the black beans, salsa, corn, bell peppers, and cilantro.
2. Serve with your favorite tortilla chips.

2 cups cooked black beans (pages 19–21), drained

16-ounce jar mild, medium, or hot salsa

1 cup cooked corn kernels

1 medium red bell pepper, cored, seeded, and finely chopped (about ¾ cup)

1 medium green bell pepper, cored, seeded, and finely chopped (about ¾ cup)

1 medium yellow bell pepper, cored, seeded, and finely chopped (about ¾ cup)

⅓ cup freshly chopped cilantro

Tortilla chips

southwestern appetizer

This is one of Joanne's family's favorites.

6 servings

1. Heat the oil in a small skillet. Add the onion and sauté until golden, stirring constantly, about 5 minutes. Stir in the chilies. Cook over medium heat, stirring, until chilies are heated through. Remove half of mixture to a small bowl; stir the chili powder, cumin, and Tabasco into the remaining onion mixture in the skillet. Heat, stirring, 1 minute.

2. Add the beans, water, salt, and black pepper to the onion mixture in the skillet. Mash the beans with a potato masher or a fork until they are as smooth as possible. Then spoon into the bottom of a 1½-quart casserole or serving dish.

3. Peel, seed, and chop the avocado into the bowl with the remaining onion mixture. Add the lemon juice,

1 tablespoon vegetable oil

½ medium onion, chopped (about ½ cup)

1 4-ounce can green chilies, drained and sliced crosswise

1 teaspoon chili powder

1 teaspoon ground cumin

¼ teaspoon Tabasco or other hot pepper sauce

2 cups cooked pinto beans (pages 19–21), drained

⅓ cup water

Salt and freshly ground black pepper to taste

1 small ripe avocado

1 tablespoon freshly squeezed lemon juice

salt, and black pepper; mash the avocado with a potato masher or fork until mixture is as smooth as possible. Spoon the avocado mixture on top of the beans in the casserole or baking dish.

4. Spread the sour cream over the avocado mixture. Top with tomato, lettuce, and cheese. Serve with tortilla chips.

1 8-ounce container sour cream or light sour cream

1 large tomato, peeled, seeded, and diced (about 1 cup)

1 cup finely shredded iceberg lettuce

1 cup shredded jalapeño Monterey Jack cheese (about 4 ounces)

Tortilla chips

salads

There was an old person of Dean,

Who dined on one pea and one bean,

   For he said, "More than that

   Would make me too fat,"

That cautious old person of Dean.

—EDWARD LEAR, *One Hundred Nonsense Pictures and Rhymes*

black and white bean salad

A simple-to-prepare, delectable salad that will convert almost anyone into a bean lover. Combining the dressing with warm beans lets them absorb and intensify the flavors.

6 to 8 servings

1. To prepare the dressing, whisk together in a large bowl the oil, vinegar, garlic, mustard, black pepper, salt, and cumin.

2. Add the beans, bell peppers, onion, and jalapeño peppers. Mix well. Taste and adjust seasoning. Cover and refrigerate until 30 minutes before serving. Serve on lettuce, if desired.

note: *Be sure to wash your hands after handling jalapeño peppers. The pepper's volatile oils could burn your eyes.*

¾ cup olive oil

¼ cup white vinegar

1 garlic clove, minced

1 tablespoon Dijon mustard

1 teaspoon freshly ground black pepper

½ teaspoon salt

½ teaspoon ground cumin

2 cups cooked black beans (pages 19–21), still warm, drained

2 cups cooked white beans (pages 19–21), still warm, drained

2½ bell peppers, assorted colors (red, green, yellow) cored, seeded, and diced (about 2 cups)

1 medium red onion, diced (about 1 cup)

1 to 2 tablespoons jalapeño peppers to taste, seeded and finely minced (see note)

Leaf lettuce (optional)

broccoli salad chinese style

With the current focus on broccoli's healthful properties, most everyone's looking for new ways to serve it. Here's a spicy side salad combined with tofu, a soybean product, that's sure to be a hit.

6 to 8 servings

1. In a large bowl, toss together broccoli, tofu, beans, water chestnuts, and bell pepper. Refrigerate until 10 minutes before serving time.
2. Whisk together soy sauce, sesame oil, sugar, and Tabasco. Toss with vegetables and let stand 10 minutes at room temperature before serving.

1 pound fresh broccoli, blanched and chopped

1 square firm-style tofu (about 4 ounces), diced in ⅛-inch cubes

¾ cup cooked adzuki beans (pages 19–21), drained

10 fresh water chestnuts, peeled and quartered, or canned, drained, and quartered

1 medium red bell pepper, cored, seeded, and chopped (about ¾ cup)

2 tablespoons soy sauce, light preferred

2 tablespoons Oriental sesame oil

1 teaspoon sugar

¼ to ¾ teaspoon Tabasco or other hot pepper sauce, to taste

---

blanching

Blanching is the quick, partial cooking of food to set the color and stop the ripening process of vegetables such as broccoli, and also to loosen the skin of foods such as peaches and tomatoes.

To blanch, immerse the food for 1 minute in boiling water. Immediately plunge it into cold water to stop the cooking process. Keep the food submerged for at least as long as it cooked.

cassoulet salad

A chilled version of the French bistro favorite.

6 servings

1. Heat 1 tablespoon oil in a medium-sized skillet over medium heat. Add the chicken and sauté until golden on both sides, about 10 minutes. Cover and cook 10 minutes or until chicken is cooked through, stirring several times.

2. Add the garlic to the skillet and sauté until garlic is golden. Remove chicken and garlic to a medium bowl. Add the water to the skillet. Cook 1 minute, stirring to dissolve any browned-on bits. Pour the liquid from the skillet into a glass measuring cup; discard excess or add water to make ¼ cup.

3. Add the skillet liquid, the remaining oil, the vinegar, thyme, salt, and black pepper to the chicken and garlic in the bowl; stir together. Stir in beans, tomato, the pepper, and scallions. Spoon onto a bed of leaf lettuce.

4. Serve immediately at room temperature or refrigerate, covered, until 30 minutes before serving.

vegetarian variation: *Omit the chicken; add 8 ounces smoked mozzarella cut into ½-inch cubes, along with the beans.*

2 tablespoons olive oil

4 boneless chicken thighs (about 1¼ pounds) cut into ½-inch pieces

2 garlic cloves, minced

¼ cup water

¼ cup white wine vinegar

½ teaspoon dried thyme leaves

Salt and freshly ground black pepper to taste

2 cups cooked white beans (pages 19–21), drained

1 large tomato, peeled, seeded, and diced (about 1 cup)

1 large green bell pepper, cored, seeded, and chopped (about 1 cup)

2 scallions, finely chopped, (about ¼ cup)

Green or red leaf lettuce

fiesta bean salad

This delicious quick-to-prepare bean salad, with its Southwest flavor, fits perfectly on a buffet, at a picnic, or at a barbecue.

8 to 10 servings

1. In a large bowl, whisk together the oil, lime juice, chopped cilantro, cumin, salt, and pepper. Mix in the beans, bell pepper, onion, corn, and jalapeño pepper.
2. Taste and adjust seasoning. Garnish with cilantro, if desired.

note: *Be sure to wash your hands after handling jalapeño peppers. The pepper's volatile oils could burn your skin or eyes.*

½ cup olive oil

6 tablespoons freshly squeezed lime juice (from about 2 limes)

¼ cup freshly chopped cilantro

1 teaspoon ground cumin

Salt and freshly ground pepper to taste

4 cups cooked black beans (pages 19–21), still warm, drained

2 medium red bell peppers, cored, seeded, and diced (about 1½ cups)

1 medium red onion, chopped (about 1 cup)

1½ cups cooked corn kernels

1 to 2 jalapeño peppers, seeded and minced (see note)

Cilantro sprigs (optional)

lentil and walnut salad

This is the perfect accompaniment to grilled meats.

6 servings

1. In a medium bowl, whisk together the oil, vinegar, salt, and black pepper.

2. Stir in the lentils, walnuts, bell pepper, parsley, and scallion. Taste and adjust seasoning.

¼ cup vegetable oil

2 tablespoons balsamic vinegar

Salt and freshly ground black pepper to taste

3 cups cooked lentils (pages 19–21), drained

½ cup chopped walnuts

½ medium red bell pepper, cored, seeded, and finely chopped (generous ⅓ cup)

¼ cup chopped fresh parsley

1 scallion, finely chopped (about 2 tablespoons)

norwegian-style bean salad

North meets south in this classic Norwegian herring and potato dish, turned into a bean one. It's quick to make and, although it sounds like an odd combination, it's unusually delicious.

1. Combine the black-eyed peas, herring, cucumber, dill, and pepper. Taste and adjust seasoning.

2. Serve at room temperature with crisp crackers or flatbread, if desired.

2 cups cooked black-eyed peas (pages 19–21), still warm, drained

1 16-ounce jar herring bits in wine sauce, undrained

1 large cucumber, peeled, seeded, and diced (about 1½ cups)

2 tablespoons snipped fresh dill *or* 2 teaspoons dried dillweed

Freshly ground black or white pepper to taste

Crackers or flatbread (optional)

red beans and rice salad

The spicy flavors of this salad will seem to rumba through your mouth. If you want to slow down the dance, just lessen the heat by reducing the amount of Tabasco, black pepper, and cayenne.

4 to 6 servings

1. To prepare the salad dressing, in a large bowl mix the oil, vinegar, Tabasco, black pepper, cayenne, and salt. Mix in the ham, scallions, celery, and andouille, if using, and allow to stand about 10 minutes.

2. Toss in the rice and beans. Taste and adjust seasoning.

note: *To rewarm leftover rice, sprinkle each cup of rice with 1 tablespoon water, cover, and microwave on full power (100 percent) for 1 minute.*

vegetarian variation: *Omit ham and sausage.*

½ cup vegetable oil

¼ cup white vinegar

1 teaspoon Tabasco or other hot pepper sauce

½ teaspoon freshly ground black pepper

½ teaspoon cayenne (ground red) pepper

½ teaspoon salt

¾ cup finely diced ham

½ cup minced scallions (about 3 medium)

2 celery ribs, chopped (about 1⅓ cups)

½ cup diced cooked andouille or other sausage (optional)

2 cups cooked brown or white rice, still warm (see note)

2 cups cooked red or small kidney beans (pages 19–21), still warm, drained

three bean salad

This traditional recipe is sometimes made with yellow (wax) beans in place of the limas.

4 servings

1. In a medium bowl, whisk together the oil, vinegar, sugar to taste, mustard, salt, and black pepper.
2. Stir in the kidney, green, and lima beans, bell pepper, and scallions. Cover and refrigerate at least 30 minutes to marinate before serving.

¼ cup olive oil

¼ cup cider vinegar

1 to 2 tablespoons sugar

½ teaspoon dry mustard

Salt and freshly ground black pepper to taste

1 cup cooked red kidney beans, (pages 19–21), drained

1 cup cooked fresh green beans (page 22), drained

1 cup cooked fresh lima beans (pages 19–21), drained

½ medium red bell pepper, cored, seeded, and finely chopped (generous ⅓ cup)

2 scallions, finely chopped (about ¼ cup)

tuna with cannellini salad

A refreshing light entree that's a snap to prepare—especially if you stock your freezer with cooked beans.

4 servings

1. In a medium bowl, whisk together the oil, lemon juice, vinegar, parsley, scallions, garlic, oregano, salt, and pepper. Stir in the cannellini beans and tuna.

2. Serve on a bed of spinach leaves, surrounded by tomato wedges.

¼ cup olive oil

2 tablespoons fresh lemon juice

2 tablespoons white vinegar

2 tablespoons chopped fresh parsley

3 scallions, finely chopped (about ⅓ cup)

2 garlic cloves, minced

2 teaspoons dried oregano

Salt and freshly ground black pepper to taste

2 cups cooked cannellini beans (pages 19–21), drained

1 7-ounce can water packed tuna, drained and flaked

4 cups spinach leaves, rinsed and well drained

4 ripe tomatoes, cut in wedges

baked
beans

And this is good

old Boston,

  The home of the

bean and the cod,

Where the Lowells

talk only to Cabots,

  And the Cabots talk

only to God.

—John Collins Bossidy,

On the Aristocracy of

Harvard, 1910

barbecued beans

A quicker version of the beans pre-
pared by old-time chuck wagon cooks.

8 servings

1. Sauté the bacon in a 3-quart
flameproof casserole or Dutch oven
until it releases its fat and starts to
brown; remove and reserve. Drain off
and discard all but 1 tablespoon fat.
Add the onion and sauté, stirring constantly, until the onion is golden,
about 5 minutes.
2. Heat the oven to 350° F. Stir the
beans, tomato juice, ketchup, brown
sugar, vinegar, Worcestershire sauce,
chili powder, mustard, Tabasco, salt,
and black pepper into the onion mixture in the casserole. Bring to a boil
over high heat, stirring constantly.
Stir in the reserved bacon.
3. Bake, uncovered, 20 to 30 minutes
or until the beans are bubbly and the
top is crisp.

vegetarian variation: *Omit the ba-*
con. Cook the onion in 1 tablespoon
vegetable oil.

4 slices bacon, coarsely
   chopped

1 large onion, chopped
   (about 1½ cups)

4 cups cooked red or
   white kidney beans
   (pages 19–21), drained

1 cup tomato juice

½ cup ketchup

2 teaspoons firmly packed
   light brown sugar

1 tablespoon cider
   vinegar

1 tablespoon
   Worcestershire sauce

1 teaspoon chili powder

1 teaspoon dry mustard

½ teaspoon Tabasco or
   other hot pepper sauce

Salt and freshly ground
   black pepper to taste

boston baked beans

Served with brown bread, these molasses-flavored beans make a traditional New England Saturday night supper.

6 servings

1. Sauté the salt pork or bacon in a 2-quart flameproof casserole or Dutch oven until it releases its fat and starts to brown; remove and reserve. Drain off and discard all but 1 tablespoon fat. Add the onion and sauté, stirring constantly, until the onion is golden, about 5 minutes.
2. Heat the oven to 350° F. Stir the beans, water, molasses, brown sugar, mustard, salt, and pepper into the onion mixture in the casserole. Bring to a boil over high heat, stirring constantly. Stir in the reserved salt pork.
3. Bake the beans, uncovered, 20 to 30 minutes or until they are bubbly and the top is crisp.

vegetarian variation: *Omit the salt pork or bacon. Cook the onion in 1 tablespoon oil.*

¼ pound salt pork or slab bacon, coarsely chopped

1 medium onion, chopped (about 1 cup)

3 cups cooked navy beans (pages 19–21), drained

¾ cup water

¼ cup light molasses

1 tablespoon firmly packed light brown sugar

1 teaspoon dry mustard

Salt and freshly ground black pepper to taste

chutney baked beans

When served at a bean tasting while creating the recipes for this book, these beans, fragrant with sweet chutney, disappeared faster than any other dish.

4 servings

1. Heat the bacon in an ovenproof casserole over low heat until its fat is released and the bacon begins to brown. Add the onion and sauté, stirring constantly, until the onion is golden, about 5 minutes.

2. Heat the oven to 350° F. Stir in the chutney, vinegar, water, mustard, and salt. Bring to a boil, stir in the beans, return to a boil, cover, and bake 20 to 30 minutes or until they are bubbly and the top is crisp.

vegetarian variation: *Omit the bacon. Cook the onion in 1 tablespoon oil.*

¼ cup diced slab bacon

1 medium onion, chopped (about 1 cup)

⅓ cup mango chutney

¼ cup white vinegar

¼ cup water

1 tablespoon mustard

½ teaspoon salt

2 cups cooked white beans (pages 19–21), drained

slow baked ranch style beans

Most of our baked bean recipes use cooked beans to make your preparation time a snap. This one starts with soaked beans and simmers them for hours in a slow oven, or over very low heat. It's for those times when you're not in a rush. To shorten the cooking time, just use 6 cups cooked, drained beans and cook only 30 to 45 minutes.

10 to 12 servings

1. In a 4-quart saucepan or Dutch oven, combine the beans, beer, tomato sauce, and enough water to just cover the beans. Stir in the bacon, onion, garlic, chili, cayenne, mustard, and black pepper. Bring to a boil over high heat, reduce heat to low, and cover. Cook stovetop or bake in a 300° F. oven for 3 to 4 hours, until the beans are cooked through.
2. Add salt. Taste and adjust seasoning.

vegetarian variation: *Omit the bacon.*

1 pound pinto beans (pages 19–20), picked over and soaked

1 12-ounce can beer

1 8-ounce can tomato sauce

½ pound slab bacon, diced

1 medium onion, chopped (about 1 cup)

1 garlic clove, minced

1 to 2 teaspoons chili powder, to taste

¼ teaspoon cayenne (ground red) pepper

½ teaspoon dry mustard

½ teaspoon freshly ground black pepper

Salt to taste

grandma lamb's
baked beans

Joanne remembers enjoying these at family reunions when she was a child. Our thanks to her aunt, Ruth Hollenbeck, for knowing the recipe.

8 servings

1. Discard soaking water and rinse beans well in a colander. Place beans in a 5-quart saucepan or Dutch oven. Cover with water; add baking soda and bring to a boil. Discard water and rinse beans again in a colander.

2. Return beans to pan; add 8 cups water, the ham bone, cayenne pepper, and black pepper. Bring to a boil over high heat; reduce heat, cover partially with a tilted lid, and cook about 1 to 1¼ hours or until beans are tender and liquid has evaporated. Taste and salt if necessary

3. Heat oven to 350° F. Remove ham bone to platter; trim off any remaining meat and discard bone. Coarsely chop meat and stir back into beans. If using slab bacon, allow bacon to remain in beans. Turn beans into a shallow 2-quart baking dish;

1 pound marrowfat or Great Northern beans (pages 19–20), soaked

½ teaspoon baking soda (see box)

1 ham bone or ¼ pound slab bacon, coarsely chopped

¼ teaspoon cayenne (ground red) pepper

½ teaspoon freshly ground black pepper

Salt to taste

¼ pound sliced bacon

top with sliced bacon and bake, uncovered, 30 to 35 minutes or until
bubbly and bacon has browned.

baking soda

*Although we don't usually rec-
ommend the addition of baking
soda to beans during cooking, we
decided to follow the original
method and found that because of
the additional water changes, it
worked fine, preserving the in-
tegrity of the beans.*

maple baked beans

The aroma of maple fills your kitchen as these bake.

6 servings

1. Melt the butter in a 2-quart flame-proof casserole or Dutch oven over medium heat. Add the onion and sauté, stirring constantly, until it is golden, about 5 minutes

2. Heat the oven to 350° F. Stir the beans, cider, maple syrup, salt, and pepper into the onions. Bring to a boil over high heat, stirring constantly.

3. Sprinkle the maple sugar over the beans and bake, uncovered, 20 to 30 minutes or until beans are bubbly and top is crisp.

1 tablespoon butter

1 medium red onion, chopped (about 1 cup)

4 cups cooked Great Northern beans, (pages 19–21), drained

1½ cups apple cider or apple juice

¼ cup maple syrup

Salt and freshly ground black pepper to taste

2 tablespoons maple sugar granules or crumbled maple sugar candies

sweet and spicy butter beans

Butter beans are lima beans. The name butter bean refers to the smooth, buttery texture and is more often used in Europe than America. The name lima comes from the capital city of their country of origin, Peru.

4 servings

1. Heat the oil in a heavy 4-quart Dutch oven over medium heat. Add the onion and sauté, stirring constantly until golden, about 5 minutes. **2.** Heat oven to 350° F. Add the beans, stewed tomatoes, ketchup, brown sugar, Worcestershire sauce, ginger, salt, Tabasco, and cloves to the onion. Bring to a boil over high heat, stirring constantly. **3.** Bake the beans, uncovered, 20 to 30 minutes or until they are bubbly and the top is crisp.

1 tablespoon olive oil

1 small onion, chopped (about ½ cup)

3 cups cooked dry lima beans or baby lima beans (pages 19–21), drained

1 14½-ounce can stewed tomatoes

2 tablespoons ketchup

2 tablespoons firmly packed light brown sugar

1 teaspoon Worcestershire sauce

½ teaspoon ground ginger

½ teaspoon salt

¼ teaspoon Tabasco or other hot pepper sauce

⅛ teaspoon ground cloves

chili

Wish I had

time for just

one more bowl

of chili.

—Alleged dying words of

Kit Carson, 1868

chunky black bean and vegetable chili

A hearty prepare-ahead entree that makes entertaining a snap. It's hot, it's spicy, and it's full of nutrient-rich goodies.

8 to 10 servings

1. Heat the oil in a 4-quart saucepan over medium-high heat. Add the onion, bell peppers, celery, jalapeño peppers to taste, and garlic; sauté until soft, about 5 to 7 minutes. Add the black beans, chili powder, cumin, oregano, and broth. Bring to a boil, reduce the heat, cover, and simmer 45 minutes, until beans are tender.

The recipe can be made ahead until this point. Refrigerate until ready to continue.

2. Stir in the tomatoes, zucchini, and corn, and cook, covered, 5 minutes more. Taste and adjust seasonings.
3. Serve over rice.

note: *Be sure to wash your hands after handling jalapeño peppers. The peppers' volatile oils could burn your skin or eyes.*

1 teaspoon vegetable oil

1 large onion, chopped (about 1½ cups)

2½ bell peppers, assorted colors, cored, seeded, and chunked (about 2 cups)

2 ribs celery, chunked (about 2 cups)

1 to 2 tablespoons minced jalapeño peppers, seeded and minced (see note)

3 garlic cloves, minced

1 cup dry black beans, picked over and soaked (pages 19–20)

¼ cup chili powder

1 tablespoon ground cumin

2 teaspoons dried oregano

3 cups chicken or vegetable broth

1 16-ounce can crushed tomatoes

2 medium zucchini, chunked (about 2 cups)

2 cups fresh or frozen corn kernels

4 cups cooked rice

chili con carne

Chili powders vary in flavor and heat. Taste this with 2 teaspoons of chili powder and add more until it is as flavorful as you like it.

6 servings

1. Heat the oil in a 4-quart saucepan over medium-high heat. Add the beef and sauté until well browned on all sides, about 10 minutes. Add the onion, bell pepper, and garlic; sauté until onion is tender, about 5 minutes longer.

2. Stir the stewed tomatoes, 3 cups water, chili powder, cumin, oregano, salt, and black pepper into the beef mixture. Bring to a boil over high heat; reduce heat to low, cover, and cook 45 minutes to 1 hour or until the beef is tender. Add remaining water if necessary.

3. Stir beans into beef mixture; bring to a boil over high heat. Cook 3 to 5 minutes or until beans are hot through. Taste and adjust seasoning. Divide into bowls and top with cheese, scallions, and cilantro.

1 tablespoon vegetable oil

1 pound lean beef round, cut into ½-inch chunks

1 medium onion, chopped (about 1 cup)

1 medium green bell pepper, chopped (about ¾ cup)

2 garlic cloves, minced

2 14½-ounce cans stewed tomatoes

3 to 4 cups water

2 to 3 teaspoons chili powder

2 teaspoons ground cumin

½ teaspoon dried oregano leaves

Salt and freshly ground black pepper to taste

2 cups cooked kidney or other red beans (pages 19–21), drained

1 cup shredded Monterey Jack or Cheddar cheese (about 4 ounces)

4 scallions, finely chopped (about ½ cup)

2 tablespoons chopped fresh cilantro or parsley

cincinnati chili

Also called five-way chili, this unique variation on the chili theme was invented by a Macedonian restaurateur who added the spices of his homeland to the chili sauce he learned to make in Coney Island before moving to Cincinnati. There seem to be as many "authentic" recipes for this dish as there are chili restaurants in Cincinnati. Unfortunately the recipes are all a secret, so this is our own.

4 servings

1. Heat the oil in a heavy 4-quart saucepan. Add the ground beef and half the onion and sauté, stirring constantly, until the beef is lightly browned and the onion is golden, about 5 minutes. Drain off and discard any fat.

2. Add the tomatoes, tomato sauce, ketchup, brown sugar, chili powder, Worcestershire sauce, cinnamon, ginger, cumin, mustard, nutmeg, cloves, and salt to the saucepan. Bring to a boil over high heat, stirring constantly. Reduce heat to low, cover, and cook 20 minutes.

3. Meanwhile, cook spaghetti in salted water according to package directions. Drain well.

1 teaspoon olive oil

½ pound lean ground beef

1 medium onion, chopped (about 1 cup)

1 8-ounce can stewed tomatoes

1 8-ounce can tomato sauce

2 tablespoons ketchup

1 tablespoon firmly packed light brown sugar

2 to 4 teaspoons chili powder

1 teaspoon Worcestershire sauce

½ teaspoon ground cinnamon

½ teaspoon ground ginger

½ teaspoon ground cumin

½ teaspoon dry mustard

¼ teaspoon ground nutmeg

⅛ teaspoon ground cloves

Salt to taste

1 8-ounce package spaghetti

2 cups cooked red kidney beans (pages 19–21), still warm, drained

1 cup shredded yellow Cheddar cheese (about 4 ounces)

4. To make chili sauce, when beef mixture has cooked 20 minutes, carefully transfer it to a food processor or blender and process until beef is finely chopped (see note).

5. Stir ¼ cup of chili sauce into beans. Divide spaghetti onto 4 plates. Top each with a quarter of the chili sauce, beans, remaining chopped onion, and the shredded cheese.

note: *Although it is traditional for sauce to be processed, it tastes just as good when left chunky. If you don't have a processor or are in a hurry, you can skip this step.*

chili powder

Commercial chili powder varies in its composition. It is basically a mixture of ground dried chili peppers and cumin. Sometimes other herbs and spices are added, such as oregano, ginger, or cayenne pepper. Chili powders purchased in Hispanic groceries and gourmet shops may contain only ground dried chilies. They vary in heat and flavor depending upon the variety of chili they are made from and whether the chilies were roasted to heighten the flavor.

pork chili con queso

A hearty, chunky, cheese-y chili.

8 servings

1. Heat the oil in a heavy 4-quart saucepan over medium-high heat. Add the pork, onion, bell pepper, and garlic and cook, stirring, until pork is browned, about 5 minutes.

2. Add the tomatoes, chili powder, cumin, salt, and pepper and simmer, uncovered, over low heat about 1 hour. Add the beans and cook until warmed through, about 10 to 15 minutes.

3. Served topped with cheese.

1 tablespoon oil

2 pounds boneless pork, cut into 1-inch cubes

1 medium onion, coarsely chopped (about 1 cup)

1 medium green or red bell pepper, cored, seeded, and coarsely chopped (about ¾ cup)

2 garlic cloves, minced

1 28-ounce can crushed tomatoes

3 tablespoons chili powder

1 tablespoon ground cumin

1 teaspoon salt

Freshly ground black pepper to taste

2 cups cooked kidney beans (pages 19–21), drained

1½ cups shredded Cheddar cheese (about 6 ounces)

turkey and cranberry bean chili

Because boned turkey breast cooks quickly, you can make this meaty chili in a hurry.

4 servings

1. Heat the oil in a 4-quart saucepan over medium-high heat. Add the turkey and sauté until well browned on all sides, about 10 minutes. Add the bell pepper, scallions, and garlic; sauté until onion is tender, about 5 minutes longer.
2. Stir the beans, stewed tomatoes, water, chili powder, cumin, dill, salt, and pepper into the turkey mixture. Bring to a boil over high heat; reduce heat to low, cover, and cook 8 to 10 minutes or until the turkey and vegetables are tender. Taste and adjust seasoning.
3. Divide into bowls and top with dill sprigs, if desired.

1 tablespoon vegetable oil

1 pound boned turkey breast, cut into ½-inch chunks

1 medium red bell pepper, chopped (about ¾ cup)

4 scallions, finely chopped (about ½ cup)

2 garlic cloves, minced

2 cups cooked cranberry beans (pages 19–21), drained

1 15-ounce can stewed tomatoes

2 cups water

2 to 3 teaspoons chili powder

2 teaspoons ground cumin

1 tablespoon chopped fresh dill *or* 1 teaspoon dried dillweed

Salt and freshly ground black pepper to taste

Fresh dill sprigs (optional)

side dishes

Then a sentimental

passion of a

vegetable fashion

must excite

your languid spleen,

An attachment

à la Plato for

a bashful

young potato,

or a not-too-French

French bean!

—W. S. GILBERT, *Patience,*

1881

beans bretonne

Cook most any dry bean in this style of Brittany, which is redolent of tomatoes, onions, and garlic. Serve as a delicious side dish for a roast—be it chicken, lamb, or beef. Or serve as a meatless meal along with a multi-grain bread.

Make a double batch and use the leftover beans to make Cassoulet (see page 112).

10 to 12 servings

3 tablespoons butter

2 large onions, chopped (about 3 cups)

½ cup dry white wine

1 pound tomatoes, peeled, seeded, and chopped (about 2 cups), *or* 1 14½-ounce can tomatoes, drained and chopped

2 garlic cloves, minced

6 cups cooked white beans (pages 19–21), drained

Salt and freshly ground black pepper to taste

2 tablepsoons chopped fresh parsley

1. Melt the butter over medium-low heat in a heavy bottomed 2-quart saucepan. Add the onions and cook until golden, about 5 to 10 minutes. Add the wine, tomatoes, and garlic. Bring to a boil, reduce heat to low, and cook 10 to 15 minutes, until a thick sauce forms.

2. Stir in the beans, season with salt and pepper, cover, and simmer for 15 minutes. Sprinkle with parsley.

christmas bean and barley pilaf

An antique bean, now available in health food and gourmet stores, Christmas beans lend a buttery flavor to this side dish.

6 servings

1. Heat the oil in a heavy 3-quart saucepan. Add the walnuts and sauté until they are lightly browned; remove to a dish and set aside. Add the onion, bell pepper, and garlic to the pan and sauté until the onion is translucent, about 3 minutes.

2. Add the barley, stir to coat with oil, then add the broth, thyme, salt, and black pepper. Bring to a boil over high heat, cover, reduce the heat to low, and cook for 30 to 40 minutes or until barley is tender.

3. Stir in the beans; cook, uncovered, 5 minutes longer or until the beans are hot and the liquid is absorbed. Taste and adjust seasoning. Turn into a serving dish and top with the reserved walnuts.

variation: *Substitute cooked fresh lima beans for the Christmas beans.*

1 tablespoon olive oil

¼ cup chopped walnuts

1 medium onion, coarsely chopped (about 1 cup)

1 medium red bell pepper, cored, seeded, and coarsely chopped (about ¾ cup)

2 garlic cloves, finely chopped

⅔ cup pearl barley

3 cups vegetable broth or water

¼ teaspoon dried thyme leaves

Salt and freshly ground black pepper to taste

2 cups cooked Christmas or large dry lima beans (pages 19–21), drained

black-eyed peas and carrots

Fresh black-eyed peas are available early in the season in some parts of the country. They are light green in color and cook quickly compared to the dry ones. If black-eyed pea snaps (immature pods) are available, they are a delicious addition to this recipe.

6 servings

1. Bring 4 cups water to a boil in a large saucepan. Add the carrots. Return to boiling; reduce heat and simmer 8 minutes or until almost tender. Add the cooked black-eyed peas (and snaps if you can find them), return to a boil, and cook 3 to 4 minutes or until carrots are tender. Drain very well and return to same saucepan.

2. Meanwhile, melt the butter in a small saucepan. Add the onion and sauté until onion is golden, about 5 minutes. In a measuring cup, combine the flour and ¾ cup water. Beat with wire whisk until well blended. Add the flour mixture to the onion in saucepan and cook, stirring constantly, until a thickened sauce forms. Stir in the salt and pepper.

3. Stir the sauce into the peas and carrots. Taste and adjust seasoning. Sprinkle with parsley or cilantro.

Water

2 medium carrots, sliced crosswise (1 cup)

2 cups cooked fresh, frozen, or dry black-eyed peas (pages 19–21)

1 cup black-eyed pea snaps (optional)

1 tablespoon butter

½ small onion, finely chopped (about ¼ cup)

1 tablespoon all-purpose flour

½ to ¾ teaspoon salt to taste

Freshly ground black pepper to taste

2 tablespoons chopped fresh parsley *or* 1 tablespoon chopped fresh cilantro

fresh beans almondine

Combining green and yellow beans adds a new look to this time-honored recipe. This is a good topping for winged beans; see page 22 for cooking instructions.

4 servings

½ pound fresh green beans

½ pound fresh yellow (wax) beans

2 tablespoons butter

¼ cup sliced natural almonds

Salt and freshly ground black pepper to taste

1. Bring 3 cups of water to boiling in a 3-quart saucepan or large skillet over high heat. Rinse beans well; snip off stem ends.

2. Add beans to boiling water; return to boiling. Cover, reduce heat, and cook 5 to 7 minutes or until just tender. Turn beans out into a colander to drain well.

3. Heat same saucepan or skillet over low heat until dry. Add butter and almonds. Cook, stirring constantly, until butter is melted and almonds just begin to turn golden. Remove from heat; add drained beans, salt, and pepper. Toss to combine; turn out into serving dish.

mixed bean and corn fritters

Any kind of cooked bean is good in this recipe. Try mixing small amounts of leftover beans of different kinds.

About 20 fritters

1. Combine the flour, cornmeal, granulated sugar, baking powder, and salt in a medium bowl. Stir in the milk and egg to make a smooth batter. Fold in the beans and corn.
2. Heat a little oil in a large skillet over medium heat. Drop the batter, a heaping measuring tablespoon at a time, into the skillet. Spread to make a 2½-inch round and fry until golden on one side. Turn and fry until golden on the other side, about 3 or 4 minutes in all. Repeat until all fritters have been fried, adding oil as needed.
3. Remove the fritters from the skillet; keep warm until all have been fried. Serve drizzled with honey or sprinkled with confectioners' sugar.

1 cup all-purpose flour

½ cup cornmeal

1 tablespoon granulated sugar

1½ teaspoons baking powder

¾ teaspoon salt

½ cup milk

1 egg

1 cup mixed cooked dry beans (pages 19–21), drained

1 cup fresh or frozen corn kernels

Vegetable oil for frying

Honey or confectioners' sugar

refried beans

Use these in any recipe calling for re-fried beans or serve them as a side dish, topping them with shredded Monterey Jack cheese just before you remove them from the heat.

4 to 6 servings

2 tablespoons oil or bacon fat

½ medium onion, finely minced (about ½ cup)

3 cups cooked pink, red, or white beans (pages 19–21), drained

Salt and freshly ground pepper to taste

Chili powder and/or ground cumin to taste (optional)

1. In a medium skillet, heat the oil over medium-high heat. Add the onion and sauté until golden, stirring constantly, about 5 minutes.

2. Add the beans, 1 cup at a time, mashing well after each addition. Season with salt, pepper, and, if desired, chili and/or cumin.

variations: *Add 1 tablespoon seeded and minced jalapeño peppers along with the onion. Or sprinkle with freshly chopped cilantro just before serving.*

red rice and lentils

A delicious accompaniment to a roast chicken, poached fish, or broiled meat—or as a hearty vegetarian entree.

4 to 6 servings

1. Heat the oil in a heavy saucepan over medium-high heat. Add the onion and bell pepper and sauté, stirring constantly, until the onion is golden, about 5 minutes. Stir in the rice, chili powder, oregano, cumin, and cayenne. Add the broth, tomatoes, and lentils; bring to a boil, reduce the heat, cover, and cook about 45 to 50 minutes, until the liquid is absorbed and the rice and lentils are tender.
2. Fluff with a fork, taste and adjust seasoning, and serve.

2 tablespoons olive oil

1 medim onion, chopped (about 1 cup)

1 medium red bell pepper, cored, seeded, and chopped (about ¾ cup)

1 cup brown rice

1 teaspoon chili powder

½ teaspoon dried oregano

½ teaspoon ground cumin

⅛ teaspoon cayenne (ground red) pepper

2 cups chicken or vegetable broth

½ cup canned crushed tomatoes

½ cup lentils

succotash

Algonquin in origin, this name meant a delicious mixture of fresh beans and corn long before European settlers came to America.

6 servings

1. Sauté the onion and bell pepper in the butter in a medium skillet over low heat until they start to brown, about 5 minutes. Add the corn and sauté, stirring constantly, until the corn is cooked through, about 10 minutes.

2. Stir in the lima beans, salt, sugar, black pepper, and thyme. Cover and cook over very low heat until the limas are heated through, about 5 to 8 minutes. Taste and adjust seasoning.

½ medium onion, finely chopped (about ½ cup)

1 small green bell pepper, finely chopped (about ½ cup)

2 teaspoons butter

1½ cups fresh corn kernels

1½ cups cooked fresh baby lima beans (pages 19–21), well drained

¼ teaspoon salt

¼ teaspoon sugar

¼ teaspoon freshly ground black pepper

⅛ teaspoon dried thyme leaves

whipped white beans and garlic

This delicious down-home alternative for mashed potatoes is a great, easy to prepare side dish with pork chops or fried chicken.

4 servings

1. Combine the beans and water to cover in a heavy 2-quart saucepan with lid. Bring to a boil over high heat and cook 5 to 10 minutes, until the beans are heated through and very soft. Drain very well and return to pan.

2. Sauté the garlic in the butter in a small skillet over low heat until it starts to brown, about 5 minutes. Turn off the heat and stir in ¼ cup milk to warm it.

3. Add the milk mixture to the cooked beans. With a hand-held electric beater, whip the beans until thoroughly pureed but not smooth, adding more milk if necessary. Stir in the salt and pepper. Taste and adjust seasoning.

4 cups cooked white beans (pages 19–21), drained

8 cloves garlic, sliced

1 teaspoon butter

½ cup milk

¼ teaspoon salt

⅛ teaspoon freshly ground black pepper

meatless main dishes

With the

bean-flowers' boon

And the

blackbird's tune,

And May, and June!

—ROBERT BROWNING, 1855

"Red beans and

ricely yours" is the

way Louis

Armstrong signed

his letters.

bean and corn quesadillas

The crunchy sweetness of fresh corn adds excitement to this easy-to-put-together treat.

8 servings

1. Slice corn kernels from cob. Combine corn, beans, cheese, chilies, cilantro, scallion, salt, black pepper, and Tabasco in a medium bowl.
2. Heat oven to 400° F. Place tortillas on a flat surface. Divide corn and bean mixture onto tortillas. Fold each tortilla in half to make a half circle; press lightly to flatten.
3. Bake 10 to 15 minutes or until filling bubbles and tortillas are golden on top. To serve, top each with a dollop of sour cream and some pepper strips.

note: *Or use ¾ cup frozen corn kernels, thawed.*

1 ear fresh corn (see note)

1 cup cooked Anasazi or Appaloosa beans (pages 19–21), drained

1 cup shredded Monterey Jack or Cheddar cheese (about 4 ounces)

2 tablespoons chopped fresh or canned green chilies

2 tablespoons chopped fresh cilantro or parsley

1 scallion, finely chopped (about 2 tablespoons)

Salt and freshly ground black pepper to taste

¼ teaspoon Tabasco or other hot pepper sauce

8 7-inch flour tortillas (1 10-ounce package)

½ to 1 cup sour cream

½ medium red bell pepper, cored, seeded, and cut into 3-inch julienne strips (about ⅓ cup)

bean burritos

Serve these flavorful bean-filled tor-tillas with rice or as part of a South-western buffet.

4 to 6 servings

1. Heat the oil in a heavy skillet over medium-high heat. Add the onion, bell pepper, jalapeño pepper, and garlic and sauté until the vegetables soften, stirring constantly, about 5 minutes. Add the tomato and cook 1 additional minute.
2. In a small bowl, partially mash the beans, using a fork. Add to skillet along with cheese, salt, and pepper and cook until warmed through, about 2 to 5 minutes.
3. Warm the tortillas, wrapped in foil, in a 350° F. oven for 10 minutes or, covered with wax paper, in the microwave on high for 30 seconds. Enclose about ¼ cup of the bean mixture in each tortilla. Serve with your favorite salsa or fresh chopped tomatoes.

note: *Be sure to wash your hands after handling jalapeño peppers. The pepper's volatile oils could burn your skin or eyes.*

1 teaspoon olive oil

1 small onion, finely chopped (about ½ cup)

1 small red bell pepper, cored, seeded, and finely chopped (about ½ cup)

1 to 2 jalapeño peppers, seeded and minced to taste (see note)

1 garlic clove, minced

1 ripe tomato, peeled, seeded, and chopped

2 cups cooked pinto, small red, or white beans (pages 19–21), drained

1 cup shredded Monterey Jack or jalapeño Jack cheese (about 4 ounces)

Salt and freshly ground black pepper to taste

6 6-inch flour tortillas

Salsa or chopped tomatoes for garnish

beans and macaroni with summer vegetables

The smoky flavor of broiled peppers, squash, and garlic turns a bowl of macaroni into a Mediterranean adventure.

6 servings

1. Combine bell peppers, zucchini, yellow squash, garlic, and oil in a medium bowl. Set aside at room temperature to marinate 30 minutes.

2. Preheat broiler. Arrange marinated vegetables on broiler pan. Set aside bowl and any remaining oil. Broil vegetables until edges are lightly browned. Turn and broil until second side is browned—about 3 to 5 minutes on each side. Cut peppers, zucchini, and yellow squash into 2-inch lengths and spoon into reserved bowl along with garlic.

3. Meanwhile, add the macaroni to salted water to cover in a heavy 2-quart saucepan. Bring to a boil over

1 medium green bell pepper, cored, seeded, and thickly sliced

1 medium red bell pepper, cored, seeded, and thickly sliced

1 medium zucchini, sliced thinly lengthwise

1 medium yellow squash, sliced thinly lengthwise

12 cloves of garlic, split

¼ cup flavorful olive oil

1 cup elbow macaroni

1 cup well-drained, cooked (pages 19–21) red or kidney beans

high heat. Reduce heat to medium and cook until macaroni is tender, about 10 to 12 minutes. Drain very well and add to vegetables along with the beans, half-and-half, 2 tablespoons Parmesan cheese, and the salt and black pepper.

4. Turn into a shallow, 2-quart flameproof casserole. Top with mozzarella cheese and remaining Parmesan. Place under broiler, 4 inches from the heat source, until cheese has melted and lightly browned.

1 cup well-drained, cooked (pages 19–21) white beans

½ cup half-and-half, warmed

¼ cup freshly grated Parmesan cheese

Salt and freshly ground black pepper to taste

½ cup shredded mozzarella cheese (about 2 ounces)

falafel

Falafel can be made with either soaked or cooked garbanzos. We feel the crunchier version made with soaked ones is worth the wait.

6 servings

1. To make Tahini, combine the sesame seeds, water, lemon juice, garlic, sugar, salt, and Tabasco in blender. Blend until a smooth sauce forms. Serve with falafel.

2. To make the falafel, combine the garbanzos, bulgur, garlic, parsley, cumin, coriander, Tabasco, salt, and black pepper in a food processor fitted with the steel blade. Process until a stiff mixture forms.

3. Divide falafel mixture into 36 balls. Roll balls between palms of hands to make round.

4. In a heavy 2-quart saucepan or deep-fryer, heat 4 inches of oil to 350° F. on deep-frying thermometer. Fry falafel balls, several at a time, 2 to 3 minutes or until golden brown on all sides. Drain well and keep warm in 275° F. oven no longer than 20 minutes.

tahini

¾ cup sesame seeds (see note)

1 cup water

1 tablespoon freshly squeezed lemon juice

1 garlic clove, sliced

1 teaspoon sugar

½ teaspoon salt

¼ teaspoon Tabasco or other hot pepper sauce

note: *You can substitute 1¼ cups prepared tahini for the sesame seeds and water.*

falafel

1 cup dry garbanzos (chick-peas), slow salt soaked 18 to 24 hours (page 19)

⅓ cup bulgur, soaked and well drained

3 garlic cloves, minced

3 tablespoons finely chopped parsley

1 teaspoon ground cumin

½ teaspoon ground coriander

5. While the falafel are frying, prepare the vegetable salad. In a small bowl, combine tomato, cucumber, bell pepper, cilantro, lemon juice, salt, black pepper, and sugar. When falafel have all been fried, divide them among the pitas. Top with the vegetable salad, shredded lettuce, and a spoonful of the Tahini. Pass remaining Tahini.

¼ teaspoon Tabasco or other hot pepper sauce

Salt and freshly ground black pepper to taste

Oil for deep-frying

vegetable salad

1 medium tomato, seeded and diced (about ¾ cup)

1 medium cucumber, peeled and diced (about ¾ cup)

½ medium green bell pepper, cored, seeded, and chopped (generous ⅓ cup)

1 tablespoon finely chopped fresh cilantro or parsley

2 teaspoons freshly squeezed lemon juice

Salt and freshly ground black pepper to taste

¼ teaspoon sugar

6 5-inch pita breads

1 cup finely shredded lettuce

pink bean and pumpkin stew

This vegetarian stew has its roots high in the Andes Mountains. Although we call for our Northern Hemisphere pumpkins or winter squash, in South America it is usually made with calabaza, a meaty, pumpkinlike squash.

6 servings

1. Combine the pumpkin with water to cover in a 3-quart saucepan. Bring to a boil over high heat. Cover and cook over low heat 15 to 20 minutes or until the pumpkin is just tender. Drain very well and set aside.

2. Heat the same saucepan over medium-high heat just until dry. Add the oil, onion, bell pepper, and garlic. Sauté until the onion is tender, about 5 minutes.

3. Stir in the stewed tomatoes, chili powder, cumin, oregano, cayenne, salt, and black pepper. Bring to a boil over high heat; reduce heat to low,

1 small pumpkin or winter squash (about 1 pound), peeled and cut into 1-inch cubes

1 tablespoon olive oil

1 medium onion, chopped (about 1 cup)

1 medium green bell pepper, chopped (about ¾ cup)

2 garlic cloves, minced

1 14½-ounce can stewed tomatoes

1 teaspoon chili powder

1 teaspoon ground cumin

¼ teaspoon dried oregano leaves

cover, and cook 10 minutes. Stir 1 cup vegetable broth into the cornmeal in a small bowl, then stir into the stew. Cook, stirring constantly, until thickened.

4. Stir the beans and pumpkin into the tomato mixture. Return to a boil; cook 3 to 5 minutes or until beans and squash are hot through, adding more broth if necessary. Taste and adjust seasoning. Divide into serving bowls; top with cilantro.

¼ teaspoon cayenne (ground red) pepper

Salt and freshly ground black pepper to taste

1 to 2 cups vegetable broth or water

2 tablespoons yellow cornmeal

2 cups cooked pink beans (pages 19–21), drained

2 tablespoons chopped fresh cilantro or parsley

To say of a man that "He knows how many beans make five," is to speak highly of his shrewdness.

—JOHN GALT, *Lawne Todd,* 1830

---

pizza provençal

White bean pizza? You bet. Topped with pesto and fresh tomatoes, this unusually delicious pie makes a hearty meal.

1 12-inch pizza to serve 4

1. Combine the water, yeast, and sugar, if desired, in a small bowl. Let stand 10 minutes to proof the yeast.
2. *By hand:* Combine the flour, basil, and salt in a large bowl. Add the yeast mixture and the oil, stirring until a soft smooth dough forms. *In a food processor fitted with the steel blade:* Combine the flour, basil, and salt by pulsing twice. Blend in half the yeast mixture with a few quick pulses. Add the rest of the yeast and the oil through the feed tube while the machine is on and operate until the mixture forms a ball of dough, about 30 to 45 seconds.
3. Turn the dough out onto a lightly floured board and knead 5 minutes, adding a bit more flour as necessary to make the dough manageable. Shape the dough into a ball and place the dough in an oiled bowl, turning to coat the dough's surface. Let rise until double in bulk, about 45 minutes to 1 hour.

pizza dough

¾ cup warm water (105° to 115° F.)

1 package active dry yeast

1 teaspoon sugar (optional)

2 to 2¼ cups all-purpose flour

2 teaspoons dried basil

1 teaspoon salt

1 tablespoon olive oil

filling

1 teaspoon oil

1 small onion, minced (about ½ cup)

2 cups cooked white beans (pages 19–21), drained

Salt and freshly ground black pepper to taste

Cornmeal

4. Meanwhile, make the filling. Heat the oil in a small skillet over medium heat. Add the onion and sauté until golden, about 5 minutes. Add the beans, mash with a fork, and season to taste with salt and pepper. Remove from heat.

5. Heat the oven to 450° F. Lightly oil a 12-inch round pan, then dust with cornmeal. Punch the dough down, remove from the bowl, and knead for 1 minute. Stretch or roll the dough into a 12-inch circle. Spread the beans over the dough, then top with the tomato slices and the pesto. Sprinkle with Parmesan.

6. Bake until the crust is browned, about 20 to 25 minutes.

variation: *Use a prebaked pizza crust. Sprinkle the basil over the fresh tomato slices and bake until pesto is bubbly and cheese melts, about 10 minutes.*

toppings

2 ripe tomatoes, sliced paper thin

¾ cup homemade (page 37) or store-bought pesto

3 tablespoons freshly grated Parmesan cheese

black bean burgers with avocado salsa

Serve as a meatless entree for dinner or on a bun for lunch.

4 servings

1 small ripe avocado

1 cup prepared salsa (page 47)

2 cups cooked black beans (pages 19–21), drained

2 tablespoons bulgur

2 tablespoons sour cream

1 scallion, finely chopped (about 2 tablespoons)

1 tablespoon finely chopped fresh cilantro or parsley

¼ teaspoon ground cumin

¼ teaspoon Tabasco or other hot pepper sauce

Salt and freshly ground black pepper to taste

Oil for frying

1. Peel, seed, and chop the avocado into a small bowl. Stir in the salsa. Cover and set aside.

2. Combine black beans, bulgur, sour cream, scallion, cilantro, cumin, Tabasco, salt, and black pepper in a food processor fitted with the steel blade. Process until mixture is well chopped but not pureed. Divide and form mixture into 4 burgers. Wrap and refrigerate burgers at least 30 minutes before cooking.

3. When ready to cook, heat oil in a heavy skillet over medium heat. Add burgers and fry 4 to 5 minutes on each side or until brown and crisp. Serve with salsa.

variations: *After turning burgers to second side, top with a slice of Monterey Jack or natural Cheddar cheese and cover skillet with a lid until cheese is melted. Or serve burgers topped with sour cream.*

ratatouille with white beans

A delicious and hearty meatless entree. Start by preparing our ratatouille recipe and add the cooked beans when the vegetables are crisp-tender.

12 to 14 servings

1. Heat the oil in a 4-quart saucepan over medium-high heat. Add the onion, garlic, and bell peppers and cook until softened, about 10 minutes. Stir in the tomatoes, eggplant, zucchini, parsley, basil, thyme, salt, and pepper. Bring to a simmer, cover, and cook over low heat for 15 minutes. Uncover and cook 5 minutes more to let thicken.

2. Stir in the beans and cook until warmed through, about 5 to 10 minutes. Taste and adjust seasoning. If desired, serve sprinkled with cheese.

2 tablespoons extra-virgin olive oil

1 large onion, chopped (about 1½ cups)

2 garlic cloves, minced

1 medium green bell pepper, cored, seeded, and chopped (about ¾ cup)

1 medium red bell pepper, cored, seeded, and chopped (about ¾ cup)

4 ripe tomatoes, peeled and chopped

1 cup canned crushed tomatoes

1 small unpared eggplant, chopped (about ¾ pound)

1 medium zucchini, cubed

¼ cup chopped fresh parsley

1 tablespoons minced fresh basil or 1 teaspoon dried

½ teaspoon dried thyme leaves

1 teaspoon salt

Freshly ground black pepper to taste

6 cups cooked white beans (pages 19–21), drained (about 1 pound)

Shredded cheese (optional)

spinach and beans with basmati rice

This is a re-creation of a favorite Afghan vegetarian entree.

4 servings

1. Cook spinach according to package directions. Drain very well.

2. Heat the oil in a medium saucepan over medium heat. Add the scallions and sauté until golden.

3. Stir the drained spinach, cumin, cinnamon, cayenne, salt, and black pepper into the scallions. In a cup, stir together water and cornstarch. Stir into spinach mixture and cook, stirring constantly, until thickened and shiny, 3 to 5 minutes.

4. Stir the beans into the spinach mixture; cook, stirring, 5 to 7 minutes or until beans are heated through.

5. Spoon the hot rice onto a serving platter. Top with the spinach and bean mixture and the peanuts. Taste and adjust seasoning.

1 10-ounce package chopped spinach

1 tablespoon peanut or other vegetable oil

2 scallions, finely chopped (about ¼ cup)

1 teaspoon ground cumin

½ teaspoon ground cinnamon

¼ teaspoon cayenne (ground red) pepper

Salt and freshly ground black pepper to taste

½ cup water

1 tablespoon cornstarch

1 cup cooked red kidney beans (pages 19–21), drained

3 cups hot, cooked basmati rice

¼ cup coarsely chopped unsalted peanuts

red beans
and rice

A vegetarian version of the tradi-
tional New Orleans Monday night
supper. Since this doesn't depend
upon the bone from Sunday's roast
ham, as the original does, you can
have it any night of the week.

6 servings

1. Heat the oil in a large, heavy skillet over medium heat; stir in flour and
cook, stirring constantly, until mixture turns caramel color, about 5 minutes. Stir in the onions, celery, bell
pepper, and garlic. Cook, stirring
constantly, until the vegetables are
lightly browned.

2. Stir tomato juice, beans, cayenne,
salt, and black pepper into vegetable
mixture. Cook, stirring occasionally,
until the beans are warmed through—
about 8 to 10 minutes. Mash some of
the beans against the side of the pan,
and stir until the mixture thickens.
Taste and adjust seasoning. Serve
over hot rice. Pass additional Tabasco.

2 tablespoons olive oil

2 tablespoons all-purpose
flour

2 medium onions,
chopped (about 2 cups)

2 celery ribs, chopped
(about 1⅓ cups)

½ medium red bell
pepper, cored, seeded,
and chopped (generous
⅓ cup)

3 garlic cloves, minced

1½ cups tomato or mixed
vegetable juice

3 cups cooked red beans
(pages 19–21), drained

½ teaspoon cayenne   — too
(ground red) pepper   much

Salt and freshly ground
black pepper to taste

3 cups hot cooked brown
or white rice

Additional Tabasco or
other hot pepper sauce

three bean curry

A quick meatless meal to make, especially if you have cooked beans on hand.

4 to 6 servings

1. Heat the butter in a medium saucepan over low heat. Add the onions and cook until golden, stirring constantly, about 5 minutes. Stir in the curry, ginger, and cumin. Then add tomato, water, beans, and peas. Bring to a boil, reduce heat, cover, and simmer until warmed through, about 5 to 10 minutes.

2. Taste and adjust seasoning. Serve over cooked rice, if desired.

4 tablespoons butter (½ stick)

2 large onions, chopped (about 3 cups)

1 to 2 tablespoons hot curry powder, to taste

½ teaspoon ground ginger

½ teaspoon ground cumin

1 large tomato, peeled, seeded, and chopped (about 1¼ cups) *or* 1¼ cups canned crush tomatoes

½ cup water

2 cups cooked garbanzos (chick-peas; pages 19–21), drained

2 cups cooked black beans (pages 19–21), drained

2 cups cooked black-eyed peas (pages 19–21), drained

Cooked rice (optional)

---

masa harina

Masa harina is a very finely ground flour made from corn that has been parched and treated with lime. It provides the characteristic flavor of tortillas, enchiladas, and other Southwestern dishes. Though regular cornmeal can be substituted for it in recipes, the flavor and texture of the final product will be quite different from the original recipe.

tamale pie

Blending tomatoes, corn, beans, and chilies always results in a winning combination. Serve this either as a light entree or as a hearty appetizer.

4 to 6 servings

1. In a medium skillet over low heat, melt butter. Add the onion and jalapeño pepper, if using, and sauté until the onion is golden, stirring constantly, about 5 minutes. Stir in the beans, corn, tomato, chili, cumin, and chilies and cook until warmed through. Remove from heat and let cool while preparing the crust.

2. Heat oven to 375° F. In a 9-inch pie plate, mix the *masa harina*, water, oil, and salt. Press evenly into the bottom and up the sides of the plate.

3. Spoon the bean mixture into the pie shell and sprinkle with cheese. Bake for 35 minutes; let stand 5 minutes before cutting.

note: *Be sure to wash your hands after handling jalapeño peppers. The pepper's volatile oils could burn your skin or eyes.*

filling

1 tablespoon butter

½ medium onion, chopped (about ½ cup)

1 jalapeño pepper, seeded and chopped (optional; see note)

1 cup cooked red beans (pages 19–21), drained

1 cup fresh or frozen corn kernels

1 medium tomato, peeled, seeded, and chopped (about 1 cup)

2 to 3 teaspoons chili powder, to taste

½ teaspoon ground cumin

1 4-ounce can green chilies, drained and chopped

crust

1¼ cups *masa harina*

⅔ cup water

2 tablespoons oil

½ teaspoon salt

1 cup Monterey Jack or Monterey Jack jalapeño cheese, shredded

rice and peas

Caribbean cooks have hundreds of different recipes for rice and peas. Some call for pigeon peas, but many use either red kidney beans or small red beans. In this quick version, the processed coconut is left with the coconut milk rather than strained out as is more common.

8 servings

1. In a blender or food processor, process the coconut and 1 cup boiling water until a smooth paste forms. Add remaining water and process until the liquid is as smooth as you can get it. Set aside.

2. Heat the vegetable oil in a 4-quart skillet or saucepan over medium heat. Add the bell peppers, scallions, and garlic and sauté until lightly browned, about 5 minutes. Stir in the coconut mixture, kidney beans, rice, salt, thyme, and Tabasco.

3. Bring mixture to a boil over high heat. Reduce heat to low, cover, and cook for 20 to 25 minutes, until liquid is absorbed and rice is tender. Taste and adjust seasoning.

note: *For an even quicker version, use packaged flaked coconut. The result will be a bit sweeter.*

1 cup shredded fresh coconut (see note)

3 cups boiling water

1 tablespoon vegetable oil

1 small green bell pepper, seeded, cored, and chopped (about ½ cup)

1 small red bell pepper, seeded, cored, and chopped (about ½ cup)

2 scallions, finely chopped (about ¼ cup)

2 cloves garlic, finely chopped

2 cups cooked red kidney beans (pages 19–21), drained

1 cup long grain white rice

½ teaspoon salt

¼ teaspoon dried thyme leaves

¼ teaspoon Tabasco or other hot red pepper sauce

sweet and sour garbanzos

Garbanzos, or chick-peas, are an Old World bean. They were being culti-vated in Mediterranean countries during Roman times.

4 servings

1. Heat the oil in a heavy 4-quart saucepan over medium heat. Add the onion and bell pepper; sauté, stirring constantly, until the onion is golden, about 5 minutes.

2. Add the pineapple with its juice, the vinegar, sugar, ketchup, ginger, salt, and Tabasco. In a measuring cup, stir the cornstarch into the water and stir into the pineapple mixture along with the garbanzos.

3. Bring to a boil over high heat, stirring constantly. Reduce heat to low, cover, and cook 8 to 10 minutes, stirring occasionally, or until beans are heated through.

1 tablespoon olive oil

1 small onion, chopped (about ½ cup)

1 small green bell pepper, cored, seeded, and chopped (about ½ cup)

1 8-ounce can crushed pineapple in juice

¼ cup cider vinegar

1½ tablespoons sugar

2 tablespoons ketchup

½ teaspoon ground ginger

¼ teaspoon salt

¼ teaspoon Tabasco or other hot pepper sauce

1 tablespoon cornstarch

1 cup water

3 cups cooked garbanzos (chick-peas; pages 19–21), drained

other main dishes

But since he stood for England

And knew what England means,

Unless you give him bacon

You must not give him beans.

—G. K. Chesterton,

The Englishman

brunswick stew

Our updated version of this old Southern favorite uses boneless thigh meat instead of a cut-up chicken. When cooked at length over low heat, boneless thighs become very tender— almost veal-like.

6 servings

1. Heat the bacon in a heavy-bottomed 2-quart saucepan over medium heat until the fat is released and the bacon is crisp. Remove bacon, crumble, and set aside.

2. Add the onion, garlic, and celery to bacon fat in saucepan, and cook, stirring occasionally, until softened, about 5 minutes. Increase heat to high and add the chicken, stirring constantly until it loses its raw look, about 5 minutes. Add lima beans, water, and Tabasco. Bring to a boil, reduce heat, cover, and let simmer 45 minutes to 1 hour, or until beans and chicken are tender.

3. Add the corn, tomatoes, Worcestershire sauce, and salt. Cook, uncovered, 10 minutes more to thicken the sauce. Taste and adjust seasoning. Serve sprinkled with parsley and the reserved bacon, if desired.

1 to 2 slices bacon

1 large onion, sliced (about 1½ cups)

2 garlic cloves, minced

2 celery ribs, chopped (about 1⅓ cups)

1½ pounds boneless chicken thighs, cut into bite-sized pieces

¾ cup baby lima beans, picked over and soaked (pages 19–20)

2½ cups water

1 tablespoon Tabasco or other hot pepper sauce

2 cups fresh or frozen corn kernels

2 large tomatoes, chopped, *or* 2 cups canned crushed tomatoes

1 tablespoon Worcestershire sauce

1 teaspoon salt

Chopped fresh parsley (optional)

brunswick stew

Brunswick Stew, originally made from squirrel or other game and onions, became famous as the preferred fare for American political rallies. In time, lima beans, tomatoes, and corn were added to the recipe and the squirrel was replaced with chicken. Several Southern counties claim to be the birthplace of this traditional dish, in a hotly debated contest that continues to this day.

entertaining with beans

We often like to entertain using a pot of beans as the center of our dinner. We might serve Three Bean Curry, Lentils and Sausages, Cassoulet, or Chunky Black Bean and Vegetable Chili (pages 104, 123, 112, 72). To complete the meal, we just add a salad, some grain—steaming rice, couscous, barley, or a crusty loaf of sourdough or other bread—and a light dessert.

We prepare the beans ahead of time, have the table set, the salad made, the bread bought or baked, and dessert ready. That gives us time to sit and enjoy our company. Now that's entertaining!

cassoulet

Originally, cassoulet was considered a peasant dish—farmers continued to add meat scraps and sausages to a pot of beans. Our cassoulet, although still a number of steps, is a simplified version of the French classic. Toss in any or a variety of favorite sausages or cooked meat to make your own rendition, with the bean as the common denominator.

12 to 15 servings

1. Heat the bacon over low heat in a large skillet until some of the fat is released and the bacon starts to brown. Increase the heat to medium. Brown the duck in the bacon fat; remove and set aside. Brown the sausage; remove and set aside. Brown the pork and lamb, if uncooked, in the bacon fat; remove and set aside.

2. In a large ovenproof casserole, layer the beans and meats, beginning and ending with the beans, seasoning each layer with salt and pepper.

½ pound thickly sliced slab bacon, diced

1 duck, about 4 to 5 pounds, cut into eight or more serving pieces

1 pound garlic or other sausage, sliced into rounds

1 pound boneless pork shoulder, cut into 2-inch cubes, *or* ¾ pound cooked lamb

1 pound boneless lamb shoulder, cut into 2-inch cubes, *or* ¾ pound cooked lamb

1 recipe Beans Bretonne (page 80)

Salt and freshly ground black pepper to taste

3. Pour off and discard the fat from the skillet. Add about a cup of water to the skillet and, over high heat, stir to loosen any browned bits stuck to the bottom of the skillet. Pour over the beans. Add enough water to almost cover the beans.

4. Bake, covered, in a 350° F. oven for 1½ to 2 hours, removing the cover for the last 15 minutes.

This can be served at this point or refrigerated overnight and reheated. Cassoulet improves with the reheating.

chicken sate

Serve this spicy peanutty chicken with steaming rice or as an appetizer.

4 to 6 servings

1. To make the marinade, combine the onion, soy sauce, brown sugar, lime juice, sesame oil, ginger, garlic, and hot pepper flakes. Pour over the chicken in a medium bowl. Cover and marinate at room temperature 45 minutes or overnight in the refrigerator.

2. To make the peanut sauce, heat the oil in a small saucepan over medium-high heat. Add the scallions and garlic and sauté until softened, about 2 minutes. Stir in the broth and peanut butter until smooth. Remove from the heat and add the soy sauce, sugar, and hot pepper flakes. Taste and adjust seasoning.

3. Heat the broiler or the grill. Thread the chicken onto skewers. Broil until cooked through, about 3 to 4 minutes per side. Serve with peanut sauce.

marinade

1 medium onion, chopped (about 1 cup)

¼ cup light soy sauce

2 tablespoons dark brown sugar

2 tablespoons fresh lime juice

1 tablespoon Oriental sesame oil

1 tablespoon minced fresh ginger

2 garlic cloves, minced

½ to 1 teaspoon hot pepper flakes

1½ pounds boneless chicken breasts, cut into 1-inch cubes

peanut butter

Instead of buying peanut butter, try making some. Place 1 cup roasted shelled peanuts in either a food processor or a blender. Add about 1 teaspoon peanut oil and ¼ teaspoon salt. Process for 2 to 3 minutes until smooth, scraping the sides of the container as needed. For chunky-style, mix about ¼ cup chopped peanuts into the peanut butter. This will make about ½ cup smooth peanut butter, ¾ cup chunky.

peanut sauce

1 teaspoon Oriental sesame oil

2 scallions, finely chopped (about ¼ cup)

2 garlic cloves, minced

½ cup chicken broth or water

⅓ cup crunchy peanut butter

2 tablespoons light soy sauce

2 teaspoons sugar

½ to 1 teaspoon hot pepper flakes, to taste

feijoada completa

Feijoada (fay-ZHWAH-dah), the national party dish of Brazil, combines black beans with a variety of meat such as beef, pork, and sausages. Brazilians serve the beans in one bowl and the meats, which usually include beef tongue and dried beef, in another. Our updated version simplifies this into a one-dish casserole and omits the tongue and dried beef.

Traditional accompaniments for feijoada include a spicy pepper sauce, bananas in a sweet butter-rum sauce, marinated onions, cooked collard greens or kale, orange slices to cool the palate, and, of course, rice. We've included two accompaniment recipes for you.

8 to 10 servings

½ cup diced salt pork or bacon

1 pound linguiça, chorizo, or other sausage, sliced

1 large onion, sliced (about 1½ cups)

1 pound boneless beef chuck, cut into 2-inch cubes

1 pound boneless country-style pork spareribs, each cut in half

1 pound black beans (pages 19–20), picked over and soaked

6 cups water

1 tablespoon vegetable oil

2 medium onions, chopped (about 2 cups)

1. Heat the salt pork over low heat in an 8- to 10-quart Dutch oven until some of the fat is released and the salt pork starts to brown. Increase the heat to medium. Add the sausages and cook until browned, about 5 minutes. Discard excess fat from the pan.
2. Add the sliced onion and cook until soft, about 5 minutes. Push to the side of the Dutch oven, add the beef cubes, and brown well. Add spareribs,

beans, and water. Bring to a boil, reduce the heat, and simmer, covered for 2 hours.

3. Just before the beans are cooked, heat the oil in a medium skillet over medium heat. Add the chopped onions, tomatoes, garlic, tabasco peppers, and parsley and cook, stirring constantly, 5 minutes, until vegetables soften. Remove 1 cup beans from the pot, add to the skillet, mash them into the vegetable mixture, and turn into the bean pot. Re-cover and cook for an additional 30 minutes, or until beans are tender. Add salt and pepper, then taste and adjust seasoning. Serve with cooked rice, Hot Onions, and Lime Pepper Sauce.

note: *Bottled tabasco peppers are available in the Spanish section of supermarkets. If unavailable, substitute 1 teaspoon Tabasco sauce for each pepper.*

2 medium tomatoes, chopped (about 1½ cups)

2 garlic cloves, minced

2 pickled tabasco peppers, drained, seeded, and finely chopped (see note)

¼ cup chopped fresh parsley

Salt and freshly ground black pepper to taste

Cooked rice

Hot Onions (recipe follows)

Lime Pepper Sauce (recipe follows)

hot onions

About ¾ cup

1. Place onion slices in a colander, pour boiling water over onions. Rinse with cold water.
2. In a small bowl, combine the Tabasco, oil, vinegar, and salt. Add the onion. Let marinate at room temperature 1 hour before serving. Serve as an accompaniment to feijoada.

1 large onion, thinly sliced (about 1½ cups)

Boiling water

2 tablespoons Tabasco or other hot pepper sauce

2 tablespoons olive oil

2 tablespoons red wine vinegar

Salt to taste

lime pepper sauce

About ¾ cup

1. In a small bowl, combine the tabasco peppers, onion, garlic, lime juice, and oil. Let marinate at room temperature 1 hour or longer in the refrigerator.
2. Serve as an accompaniment to feijoada.

note: *Bottled tabasco peppers are available in the Spanish section of supermarkets. If unavailable, substitute 1 teaspoon Tabasco sauce for each pepper.*

4 bottled tabasco peppers, drained and finely chopped (see note)

1 medium onion, chopped (about 1 cup)

2 garlic cloves, minced

½ cup fresh lime juice

3 tablespoons olive oil

grandma leese's hominy and beans

Joanne's mother remembers coming home from school at lunchtime to a steaming plate of hominy and beans. It was usually made with the speckled beans they grew in the garden, but kidney beans make a good alternative.

4 servings

1. Cook the bacon in a large skillet over medium heat, until it releases its fat and is crisp. Remove bacon and set aside. Discard all but 2 tablespoons bacon fat from the skillet.

2. Add the onion to the reserved bacon fat in the skillet and sauté until golden, stirring constantly, about 5 minutes.

3. Add the beans and hominy; cook, stirring, until they are heated through, about 5 minutes. Add salt and pepper. Serve sprinkled with the reserved bacon.

2 strips bacon, cut into 1-inch pieces

½ medium onion, finely chopped (about ½ cup)

2 cups cooked red or white kidney beans (pages 19–21), drained

2 cups cooked or canned hominy, well drained

Salt and freshly ground black pepper to taste

ham steak
with beans and
potatoes

A one-dish meal for busy evenings.

4 servings

1. Heat the oil in a large heavy skillet over medium heat. Brown the ham steak in the oil lightly on both sides. **2.** Add the water and potatoes; cover and cook 10 minutes. Add all the beans, salt, and pepper; cover and cook 10 minutes longer or until the potatoes and fresh beans are tender. Check water occasionally and add more if needed. Taste and adjust seasoning and serve.

1 teaspoon vegetable oil

1-pound fully cooked ham steak

2 cups water

2 large potatoes, peeled and quartered lengthwise

¼ pound fresh green beans

¼ pound fresh yellow (wax) beans

1 cup cooked red kidney beans (pages 19–21), drained

Salt and freshly ground black pepper to taste

120

hoppin' john

This is a super spicy version of a Southern favorite that's customarily served on New Year's Day. To lessen the heat a tad, reduce or eliminate the hot sauce.

4 to 6 servings

1. Heat the oil in a heavy-bottomed 2-quart ovenproof casserole over medium heat. Add the sausage and stir occasionally until cooked, about 3 minutes. Add the onion and garlic and sauté, stirring frequently, until the onion is golden, about 5 minutes.
2. Add to the casserole the black-eyed peas, brown rice, wild rice, Tabasco, if using, salt, cayenne, and water.
3. Heat oven to 350° F. Bring casserole ingredients to a boil over high heat. Cover and bake in oven 50 to 60 minutes, or until peas and rice are tender and all the liquid is absorbed. Fluff with a fork, taste and adjust seasoning, and serve sprinkled with parsley, if desired.

note: *Instead of baking in the oven, you can cook stovetop over low heat for the same amount of time.*

vegetarian variation: *Omit the sausage.*

1 teaspoon olive oil

¾ cup diced andouille or other smoked pork sausage (about 4 ounces)

1 medium onion, sliced (about 1 cup)

2 garlic cloves, minced

¾ cup dry black-eyed peas, picked over and rinsed

½ cup brown rice

¼ cup wild rice

1 teaspoon Tabasco or other hot pepper sauce (optional)

1 teaspoon salt

¼ teaspoon cayenne (ground red) pepper

3½ cups water

Chopped fresh parsley (optional)

lamb and white bean stew

Simple to prepare ahead and serve for company.

4 servings

1. Heat the oil in a heavy 4-quart saucepan over medium-high heat. Add the lamb cubes and brown. Remove and set aside.

2. Add the onion and sauté until it is golden, stirring constantly, about 5 minutes. Add the tomatoes, parsley, and garlic and cook an additional 3 minutes.

3. Return lamb to pan. Add the water and beans. Bring to a boil over high heat, reduce the heat to low, cover, and simmer for 1 hour or until the lamb is tender. Add salt and pepper. Taste and adjust seasoning.

2 teaspoons oil

1 pound boneless lamb, cut into 1-inch cubes

1 large onion, sliced (about 1½ cups)

4 medium ripe tomatoes, peeled, seeded, and diced (about 4 cups), *or* 1 28-ounce can crushed tomatoes, well drained

½ cup chopped fresh parsley

2 garlic cloves, minced

2 cups water

2 cups cooked white beans (pages 19–21), drained

Salt and freshly ground black pepper to taste

lentils and sausages

A quick, hearty, stick-to-your ribs en-
tree. Serve with a bowl of steaming
hot rice, couscous, or barley.

4 servings

1. In a heavy skillet, sauté the sausage until thoroughly cooked, about 3
to 5 minutes. Remove from skillet to
paper toweling and set aside. Remove
all but 2 tablespoons of fat from skillet.

2. Add onions and garlic to skillet and sauté until tender but not
browned, about 5 minutes. Add the
broth, lentils, vinegar, oregano, and
bay leaf. Bring to a boil, reduce heat,
and simmer 10 minutes. Add tomatoes and zucchini, cover, and continue
to simmer 15 minutes or until lentils
are tender.

3. Return the sausage to the skillet,
add salt and pepper to taste, and simmer 5 minutes, or until the sausage is
heated through.

4. Serve sprinkled with minced parsley, if desired.

1 pound andouille,
   chorizo, or Italian hot
   sausage, sliced

2 medium onions, minced
   (about 2 cups)

2 garlic cloves, minced

3 cups chicken broth

½ pound lentils, picked
   over and rinsed (about
   2 cups)

2 tablespoons wine
   vinegar

1 teaspoon dried oregano

1 bay leaf

1 28-ounce can plum
   tomatoes, undrained

2 medium zucchini, cut
   into ¼-inch-thick slices
   (about 2½ cups)

¼ teaspoon or more salt

¼ teaspoon or more
   freshly ground black
   pepper

Freshly minced parsley
   (optional)

shrimp in black bean sauce

An unusual variation of an Oriental classic.

2 servings

1. In a small bowl, partially mash half the beans, using a fork.
2. Heat the oil in a wok or skillet over high heat. Add ginger and garlic; toss 1 minute. Add the beans, shrimp, and ½ cup water. Cover and cook 2 minutes, until the shrimp are almost cooked and firm to the touch.
3. Mix the cornstarch with 1 tablespoon water. Remove cover from skillet; stir in the cornstarch mixture and soy sauce. Cook until sauce thickens, about 1 to 2 minutes. Remove from heat.
4. Sprinkle with scallions and serve over rice.

1 cup cooked black beans (pages 19–21), drained

1 tablespoon oil

1 tablespoon minced fresh ginger

3 garlic cloves, minced

¾ pound peeled and deveined shrimp

Water

1 teaspoon cornstarch

1 tablespoon light soy sauce

2 scallions, minced

1 cup hot, cooked rice

spanish rice and beans

A tasty accompaniment to any entree. Or for an interesting combination, serve smothered with a favorite chili such as Pork Chili con Queso (page 76) or Chunky Black Bean and Vegetable Chili (page 72).

4 to 6 servings

1. Heat the oil in a heavy-bottomed 2-quart saucepan over medium heat. Add the pork and heat until cooked through. Add onion, bell pepper, and garlic. Sauté until the vegetables soften, stirring constantly, about 5 minutes. Add the rice, stir to coat with the oil, and cook until golden, about 2 minutes.
2. Stir in the broth, saffron, garbanzos, tomato, salt, and pepper. Bring to a boil, reduce the heat, cover, and simmer 20 to 25 minutes, until the rice is tender and the liquid is absorbed. Remove from heat, fluff with a fork, and serve.

vegetarian variation: *Omit the salt pork. Use vegetable broth or water.*

1 teaspoon olive oil

½ cup diced salt pork or slab bacon

1 medium onion, finely chopped (about 1 cup)

1 medium red bell pepper, cored, seeded, and finely chopped (about ¾ cup)

2 garlic cloves, minced

1 cup white rice

2 cups chicken or vegetable broth or water

½ teaspoon saffron threads

1½ cups cooked garbanzos (chick-peas; pages 19–21), drained

1 medium tomato, peeled, seeded, and diced (about ¾ cup), *or* ¾ cup canned crushed tomatoes

Salt and freshly ground black pepper to taste

tamale pie too

This version of tamale pie has appeared in women's magazines since the 1930s.

4 to 6 Servings

1. In a medium skillet with oven-proof handle, heat the oil over medium heat. Add the ground beef, onion, and bell pepper. Cook, stirring occasionally, until the meat is no longer pink and the vegetables have begun to brown, about 8 to 10 minutes.

2. Stir in the stewed tomatoes, beans, water, cornmeal, chili powder, and cumin. Cook, stirring, until mixture comes to a boil and thickens slightly, about 8 to 10 minutes.

3. Heat oven to 375° F. Combine the cornmeal, flour, baking powder, sugar, and salt in a medium bowl. Add the milk, egg, and oil. Stir together with a fork just until moistened. Spoon over chili mixture and bake 25 to 30 minutes or until topping is baked through.

vegetarian variation: *Substitute 8 ounces firm tofu, crumbled, for the beef. Stir in with tomatoes in Step 2.*

filling

1 tablespoon vegetable oil

½ pound ground beef or turkey

½ medium onion, chopped (about ½ cup)

½ medium green bell pepper, cored, seeded, and chopped (generous ⅓ cup)

1 15-ounce can stewed tomatoes

1½ cups cooked red beans (pages 19–21), drained

½ cup water

2 tablespoons cornmeal

1 to 2 teaspoons chili powder

1 teaspoon ground cumin

topping

½ cup yellow cornmeal

½ cup all-purpose flour

1½ teaspoons baking powder

1 teaspoon sugar

¼ teaspoon salt

½ cup milk

1 egg

2 tablespoons vegetable oil

teriyaki chicken and bean sprouts

Although most commercial bean sprouts are mung beans, soybeans and adzuki beans make delicious sprouts as well. (See page 128 for instructions on sprouting at home.)

4 servings

1. In a medium bowl, combine soy sauce, sherry, corn syrup, and ginger. Set aside.

2. Heat the oil in a large skillet over medium heat. Add the chicken pieces; sauté until browned on both sides, 6 to 8 minutes.

3. Stir in the bean sprouts, snow peas, bell pepper, and scallions. Stir-fry 5 minutes. Stir in the soy sauce mixture and beans; cook 5 minutes longer or until vegetables are crisp-tender.

4. To serve, spoon vegetable mixture over hot rice.

2 tablespoons soy sauce

2 tablespoons cream sherry

2 tablespoons light corn syrup

1 tablespoon minced fresh ginger

1 tablespoon vegetable oil

4 boned and skinned chicken breast halves (1 pound), cut into 1-inch cubes

2 cups fresh bean sprouts

¼ pound snow peas, stems removed

½ medium red bell pepper, cored, seeded, and thinly sliced into strips (generous ⅓ cup)

2 scallions, finely chopped (about ¼ cup)

1 cup cooked adzuki beans (pages 19–21), drained

2 cups hot, cooked rice

sprouting at home

You can just as easily prepare bean sprouts at home. To do so:

1. Select edible, organic beans. Don't use beans intended for planting because they may have been treated with chemicals. Sprouting mixes are available in health food stores or by mail from Walnut Acres (see Mail Order Sources).

2. Pick over and rinse beans well. Place ¼ cup beans in a quart jar. Fill with water to within 2 inches of top of jar. Cover top of jar with several layers of cheesecloth secured with canning ring or a rubber band. Let stand at room temperature overnight.

3. Next day, without removing the cheesecloth, drain beans and rinse well. Let jar stand upside down 30 minutes to remove excess moisture, then place on its side in a warm, dark place for 3 to 4 days until sprouts reach desired length. Rinse and drain well several times each day. If any mold appears, discard the moldy sprouts.

4. Just before using, allow sprouts to stand in sunlight for 1 hour to become green. Rinse well and serve. Mung bean and lentil sprouts can be eaten raw. Other sprouts such as soybean must be cooked before eating for better digestion.

5. If desired, a sprouting container is available from Walnut Acres (see Mail Order Sources).

desserts

Full o' beans and

benevolence!

—Robert Smith Surtees,

Hanley Cross, 1843

chocolate peanut butter pie

Although often used in the same way as nuts, peanuts are clearly legumes. The complementary flavors of chocolate and peanut make this pie dangerously habit-forming.

6 servings

1. With fingers or a fork, combine ⅔ cup confectioners' sugar and the peanut butter in a small bowl to make coarse crumbs.

2. Stir together the granulated sugar, cornstarch, and salt in a 2-quart saucepan. Gradually stir in the eggs and milk. Bring the mixture to a boil over low heat and cook about 5 minutes, stirring constantly. Stir in the chocolate; cook, stirring, until the chocolate melts and the pudding is thick and smooth. Stir in the vanilla.

3. Sprinkle a third of the peanut butter crumbs into the bottom of the pie shell. Top with half of the chocolate pudding. Sprinkle with another third of the crumbs and top with the remaining pudding. Reserve remaining crumbs. Cool pie completely; then refrigerate, covered, until thoroughly chilled—at least 2 hours.

⅔ cup plus 2 tablespoons confectioners' sugar

½ cup chunky peanut butter (page 115)

¾ cup granulated sugar

¼ cup cornstarch

¼ teaspoon salt

2 eggs

3 cups milk

3 ounces unsweetened chocolate

2 teaspoons vanilla extract

1 9-inch baked pie shell (recipe follows)

1 cup (½ pint) heavy cream

¼ cup coarsely chopped unsalted peanuts

4. When the pie is chilled, with an electric mixer, whip the heavy cream and the remaining 2 tablespoons confectioners' sugar until stiff. Spoon the whipped cream evenly over top of pie. Sprinkle the remaining crumbs and the peanuts over the cream. Cover and store in the refrigerator until ready to serve.

pie shell

To make a two-crust pie, double this recipe and roll out into two 11-inch rounds or use as directed in recipe.

1. In a medium bowl, combine the flour, salt, and sugar. With a pastry blender or two knives, cut in the butter and shortening until the mixture resembles coarse crumbs.

2. With a fork, stir in ¼ cup water until the mixture forms a ball of dough. Add a little more water, if necessary, to make the dough manageable.

3. Shape dough into a flattened ball and roll out between pieces of wax paper to make an 11-inch round. Fit into a 9-inch pie plate and crimp edges. Fill and bake as directed in pie recipe. Or for baked pie shell, preheat oven to 375°F. Pierce bottom and side of shell with tines of fork. Bake for 5 to 10 minutes or until golden.

For one 9-inch shell:

1½ cups all-purpose flour

½ teaspoon salt

½ teaspoon sugar

4 tablespoons butter (½ stick)

2 tablespoons vegetable shortening

Cold water

holiday bean pie

Don't be surprised if this Southern regional pie becomes a family favorite—it tastes very much like sweet potato or pumpkin pie.

8 servings

1. Heat oven to 375° F. Combine the beans, brown sugar, half-and-half, egg, flour, cinnamon, ½ teaspoon nutmeg, and the vanilla in a food processor with the steel blade attached or in a blender. Process until smooth. Pour the mixture into the prepared pie shell and sprinkle with additional nutmeg.
2. Bake 40 to 45 minutes or until the top is lightly browned and the center is set. Cool on wire rack for 30 minutes. Serve warm, or cool completely and refrigerate to serve chilled. Serve each portion topped with a spoonful of whipped cream.

2 cups cooked white beans (pages 19–21), well-drained

½ cup firmly packed light brown sugar

1 cup half-and-half

1 egg

1 tablespoon all-purpose flour

2 teaspoons ground cinnamon

½ teaspoon freshly grated nutmeg

½ teaspoon vanilla extract

1 9-inch pie shell (page 131), unbaked

Additional nutmeg for garnish

Sweetened whipped cream

red bean and apple dumplings

Inspired by Chinese steamed red bean dumplings and American apple dumplings, this is a surprisingly delicious combination.

6 servings

1. Prepare the pastry. Set aside, covered.

2. Melt the butter in a large skillet over medium heat. Add the apple slices and cook, turning frequently, until tender and lightly browned.

3. Stir in beans, sugar, and ginger. Cook 5 minutes, or until beans are heated through. With a spoon, mash beans as they cook. Turn filling out onto a plate to cool.

4. Heat oven to 400° F. Divide the reserved pastry into 6 pieces. Roll each piece out to make a 6-inch round. Divide the filling onto pastry rounds. To shape the dumplings, lift side of pastry round and pinch together in the center. Place, pinched side down, on an ungreased baking sheet. Pierce the top with the tines of a fork.

5. Bake 25 to 30 minutes or until pastry is golden brown. Let cool at least 20 minutes before serving. Serve with vanilla ice cream or sweetened whipped cream, if desired.

Pastry for double-crust pie (page 131)

1 tablespoon butter

1 large Granny Smith or other tart apple, peeled, cored, and thinly sliced

1½ cups cooked red beans (pages 19–21), drained

3 tablespoons sugar

2 tablespoons finely chopped crystallized ginger

Vanilla ice cream or sweetened whipped cream (optional)

133

white bean
ice milk

Don't laugh! Beans give body and creaminess to this fat- and cholesterol-free dessert.

8 servings (about 1 quart)

1. Combine the gelatin with ½ cup of the milk in a glass measuring cup. Set aside 5 minutes to soften. When gelatin has softened, place the cup in a saucepan of hot but not boiling water. Stir until gelatin is dissolved.

2. Meanwhile, process the beans and the remaining ½ cup milk in a food processor fitted with a cutting blade (or in several batches in a blender), until very smooth. Stir in the gelatin mixture, sugar, vanilla, and salt.

3. To make ice milk, turn the bean mixture into the container of a 1-quart ice-cream maker and process according to manufacturer's directions. If you don't have an ice-cream maker, turn into a 13 by 9-inch baking pan; cover tightly and place in the freezer for 2 or 3 hours, until slushy but not firm. Remove to a large bowl and whip with a heavy-duty electric mixer until smooth and fluffy. Pack into freezer containers and freeze until ready to serve.

1 envelope unflavored gelatin

1 cup skim milk

4 cups cooked Great Northern or white kidney beans (pages 19–21), well-drained

⅓ cup sugar

2 tablespoons vanilla extract

¼ teaspoon salt

mail order

sources

Balducci's
424 Avenue of the Americas
New York, NY 10011
(212) 673-2600
Visit their New York store or call
for a mail order catalogue.

Dean & DeLuca
560 Broadway
New York, NY 10012
(212) 431-1691
1-800-221-7714 (outside New
York City)
Large selection of unusual beans.
Visit their New York store or call
for a mail order catalogue.

Pete's Spice and Everything Nice
174 First Ave.
New York, NY 10003
(212) 254-8773
Personal service. Call and see
what's in stock.

Shiloh Farms
P.O. Box 97
Benton County
Sulphur Springs, AR 72768-0097
(501) 298-9631 or 3359
Available in health food stores or
by mail.

Walnut Acres
Penns Creek, PA 17862
1-800-433-3998
Call for a mail order catalogue.

index

Page numbers in **boldface** refer to text in boxes.

Conversions

Equivalent Imperial and Metric Measurements

American cooks use standard containers, the 8-ounce cup and a tablespoon that takes exactly 16 level fillings to fill that cup level. Measuring by cup makes it very difficult to give weight equivalents, as a cup of densely packed butter will weigh considerably more than a cup of flour. The easiest way therefore to deal with cup measurements in recipes is to take the amount by volume rather than by weight. Thus the equation reads:

1 cup = 240 ml = 8 fl. oz.   ½ cup = 120 ml = 4 fl. oz.

It is possible to buy a set of American cup measures in major stores around the world.

In the States, butter is often measured in sticks. One stick is the equivalent of 8 tablespoons. One tablespoon of butter is therefore the equivalent to ½ ounce/14 grams.

Liquid Measures

Fluid ounces	U.S. measures	Imperial measures	Millimeters
	1 tsp	1 tsp	5
	2 tsp	1 dessertspoon	10
½	1 tbs	1 tbs	14
1	2 tbs	2 tbs	28
2	¼ cup	4 tbs	56
4	½ cup		110
5		¼ pint or 1 gill	140
6	¾ cup		170
8	1 cup		225
9			250 or ¼ liter
10	1¼ cups	½ pint	280
12	1½ cups		340
15		¾ pint	420
16	2 cups		450
18	2¼ cups		500 or ½ liter
20	2½ cups	1 pint	560
24	3 cups		675
25		1¼ pints	700
27	3½ cups		750
30	3¾ cups	1½ pints	840
32	4 cups or 1 quart		900
35		1¾ pints	980
36	4½ cups		1000 or 1 liter
40	5 cups	2 pints or 1 quart	1120
48	6 cups		1350
50		2½ pints	1400
60	7½ cups	3 pints	1680
64	8 cups or 2 quarts		1800
72	9 cups		2000 or 2 liters
80	10 cups	4 pints	2250
96	12 cups or 3 quarts		2700
100		5 pints	2800

Solid Measures

U.S. and Imperial measures		Metric measures	
ounces	pounds	grams	kilos
1		28	
2		56	
3½		100	
4	¼	112	
5		140	
6		168	
8	½	225	
9		250	¼
12	¾	340	
16	1	450	
18		500	½
20	1¼	560	
24	1½	675	
27		750	¾
28	1¾	780	
32	2	900	
36	2¼	1000	1
40	2½	1100	
48	3	1350	
54		1500	1½
64	4	1800	
72	4½	2000	2
80	5	2250	2¼
90		2500	2½
100	6	2800	2¾

Suggested Equivalents and Substitutes for Ingredients

all purpose flour—plain flour
coarse salt—kitchen salt
confectioners' sugar—icing sugar
cornstarch—cornflour
granulated sugar—caster sugar
sour cherry—morello cherry
unbleached flour—strong, white flour
vanilla bean—vanilla pod
zest—rind
heavy cream—double cream
baking sheet—oven tray
cheesecloth—muslin
parchment paper—greaseproof paper
plastic wrap—cling film

Oven Temperature Equivalents

Fahrenheit	Celsius	Gas Mark	Description
225	110	¼	Cool
250	130	½	
275	140	1	Very Slow
300	150	2	
325	170	3	Slow
350	180	4	Moderate
375	190	5	
400	200	6	Moderately Hot
425	220	7	Fairly Hot
450	230	8	Hot
475	240	9	Very Hot
500	250	10	Extremely Hot

Any broiling recipes can be used with the grill of the oven, but beware of high-temperature grills.